"The absolute last thing that most parents need is more pressure. That's why I'm so glad that Adam Griffin wrote something different—a book full of grace and relief for parents. I trust his voice to encourage families by helping them see how much their faith can bless them and their God can unburden them."

Matt Chandler, Lead Pastor, The Village Church, Flower Mound, Texas

"*Good News for Parents* offers wise remedies for the inevitable fears parents face. This book is not a list of *how-tos* but a biblical vision of *how God* provides the guidance we need. Through a careful explanation of the fruit of the Spirit, enriched with poems and prayers, Adam Griffin helps us relax and trust Christ with the results of our parenting. His message is clear: We are not the center of it all—Jesus is. And that is truly good news for every parent!"

Ray and Jani Ortlund, President and Executive Vice President, Renewal Ministries

"In *Good News for Parents*, Adam Griffin offers relief for those stuck in a loop of self-sufficient striving to 'ace' the parenting test and the shame that comes from inevitably falling short. Griffin intentionally avoids formulas, techniques, and checklists in order to point readers to something much better: a Spirit-empowered, gospel-saturated parenthood flowing out of parents' identity as beloved children of God. I recommend this book for moms and dads in need of gospel refreshment!"

Caroline Cobb, singer-songwriter; author, *Advent for Exiles*

"There is no shortage of good advice for parents, and Adam Griffin has offered some of the best out there. But in this book we don't just get something helpful; we receive something better: good news for parents. Good news for faithful parents, good news for failing parents, good news for fatigued parents—good news for us all."

Kyle Worley, Pastor, Mosaic Church, Richardson, Texas; author, *Home with God: Our Union with Christ*; Cohost, *Knowing Faith* podcast

"In *Good News for Parents*, Adam Griffin takes us on a gospel-centered journey, rich with Scripture and story, revealing how God can transform both the parent and the very atmosphere of the home! Using the fruit of the Spirit from the book of Galatians, Griffin helps us see how a house filled with stress, despair, and anxiety can be changed into a home full of unending love, joy, peace, and—dare I say—the very presence of God himself! What follower of Jesus wouldn't want that?"

Phil and Diane Comer, Cofounders, Intentional Parents International

"There is real grace on every page of this book. If you, like me, are a parent who veers between feeling proud, complacent, overwhelmed, and crushed, this realistic yet hope-filled book will root you in the goodness of Jesus and show you how his Spirit really does enable you to be the parent you'd like to be. Chapter by chapter, Griffin showed me how to be a better dad, but even more than that, he showed me how to enjoy having a perfect Father."

Carl Laferton, author, *The Garden, the Curtain, and the Cross* and *God's Big Promises Bible Storybook*

"After reading this book, I have a word to describe it that I've never used for a parenting book: *refreshing*. Sometimes books on parenting make me anxious, or I come away feeling less confident. Not this one! Adam Griffin is a great writer and storyteller, and his book is practical, insightful, and authentic. Griffin is a pastor who gives us a biblical but not 'preachy' way to look at our most important role."

Jim Burns, Founder, HomeWord; author, *A Student's Guide to Sexual Integrity* and *Doing Life with Your Adult Children*

"I was literally clapping my hands as I read this book, applauding the way it provides grace-filled, Holy Spirit–focused encouragement for parents! What an incredible relief to know that we have both the powerful presence of the Holy Spirit and the gift of grace to carry us as we raise our children to follow Jesus. This is an incredible resource for young parents to provide them with a Christ-centered vision for their parenting journey. I am confident that you will be empowered as you apply these profound truths to your parenting."

Jason Houser, Founder, Seeds Kids Worship; coauthor, *Dedicated: Training Your Children to Trust and Follow Jesus*

"*Good News for Parents* offers relief to parents struggling with anxiety and shame by ushering them into the rest the gospel provides. Adam Griffin helps moms and dads apply the gospel to various parenting challenges, empowering readers to parent as though they really have been saved by grace. This book is a breath of fresh air!"

Hunter Beless, author; Founder, Journeywomen Ministries

Good News for Parents

Good News for Parents

How God Can Restore Our Joy
and Relieve Our Burdens

Adam Griffin

WHEATON, ILLINOIS

Good News for Parents: How God Can Restore Our Joy and Relieve Our Burdens

© 2025 by Adam Griffin

Published by Crossway
          1300 Crescent Street
          Wheaton, Illinois 60187

All hymns used as epigraphs in the book are in the public domain.

Cover design and images: David Fassett

First printing 2025

Printed in the United States of America

Hardcover ISBN: 978-1-4335-9772-5
ePub ISBN: 978-1-4335-9774-9
PDF ISBN: 978-1-4335-9773-2

Library of Congress Cataloging-in-Publication Data

Names: Griffin, Adam, author.
Title: Good news for parents : how God can restore our joy and relieve our burdens / Adam Griffin.
Description: Wheaton, Illinois : Crossway, [2025] | Includes bibliographical references and index.
Identifiers: LCCN 2024050724 (print) | LCCN 2024050725 (ebook) | ISBN 9781433597725 (hardcover) | ISBN 9781433597732 (pdf) | ISBN 9781433597749 (epub)
Subjects: LCSH: Parents—Religious life. | Parenting—Religious aspects—Christianity.
Classification: LCC BV4529 .G737 2025 (print) | LCC BV4529 (ebook) | DDC 248.8/45—dc23/eng/20250319
LC record available at https://lccn.loc.gov/2024050724
LC ebook record available at https://lccn.loc.gov/2024050725

Crossway is a publishing ministry of Good News Publishers.

VP			34	33	32	31	30	29	28	27	26	25
15	14	13	12	11	10	9	8	7	6	5	4	3	2	1

This work is dedicated to our many dear friends who struggle with how they feel about their parenting. This is for all the discouraged, the overwhelmed, and the exhausted moms and dads my wife and I talk to all the time. We love you. You are more cherished and secure in the arms of God than you could know.

Contents

Acknowledgments

MY WIFE, CHELSEA, and our three boys should be the first to be acknowledged. If there's anything worth reading here, it is probably something I learned from watching my wife follow Jesus and lead our kids so well. As for our boys, I know it often feels as if they endure added, unfair scrutiny because I talk so much to other people about parenting, and for that, Oscar, Gus, and Theodore deserve some significant acknowledgment (and some ice cream). I am an unusual dad trying to raise uncommon kids, and that doesn't make their life any easier. Sons, thank you for putting up with so much and being a non-stop blessing to me.

Much of this book was written over two separate week-long writing vacations and a series of Friday mornings off from pastoring. Glossers and Masons, I am so grateful for the space to write that you provided at your beautiful lake house. Paige and Tyler, so much of this book came from the time you afforded me there. I'm truly indebted and grateful.

For partnering with me on that first writing retreat, I must thank Kyle Worley. Kyle, you are a dear friend, and you give great feedback and encouragement. In a hundred ways, this book would not have happened without you.

All the finishing touches to this book were written at Cross Creek Ranch overlooking Lake Whitney, south of Dallas. Thank you, Hawkins and Boutros families, for creating a space that cultivates so much peace.

Chelsea and I were so blessed to be there as we completed this work. Johnny, Momsy, Victor, and Virginia—your friendship and generosity has meant so much to my family.

On my Friday mornings off from my regular pastoring duties at Eastside Community Church, I often slid down to my favorite neighborhood coffeeshop, Civil Pour, to write. If any part of this book seems particularly upbeat, it was probably written after downing one of their delicious hot mochas. I'm grateful for their cheery staff, who would show genuine interest in how writing was going (and even let me sneak in before opening sometimes).

Though he's not alive to read this acknowledgment, Charles Haddon Spurgeon has often been an inspiration to me as a pastor, preacher, author, and father. Each chapter is prefaced by a hymn I found in *Spurgeon's Hymnal* or the "Songs and Hymns" from his *Home Worship and the Use of the Bible in the Home*. I reread these hymns many times while trying to get my heart and mind in the right place to write each chapter.

To the elders and staff of Eastside, who encourage me to write, humble me as a leader, care for me as a man, and bless me beyond words, I could not be more thankful. Our ministry together is a true gift.

Erik, thank you for being the kind of agent who cuts through my insecurities and says what I need to hear to keep working. You're a gift to all your clients.

To my beta readers (Kyle, Kelly, Marissa, Mary, Sami, Kimi, Kendall, Lane, and Chelsea), this book is so much better because you took the time to read it and tweak it. Your time and your support mean so much to me.

And lastly, I want to acknowledge you, readers. It's for you that I write. I hope this blesses you. I want these words to be more than true. I want them to be helpful.

God bless our home forever,
And all our loved ones there!
May no unkindness sever
The hearts so true and fair!

O, may its light so loving
Shine brightly 'mid the dark,
To lure from sin and roving
Our sad, world-weary bark!

Home, home; sweet, sweet home!
God bless our home forever,
Sweet heav'n is mirrored there!

God bless our home where nightly
We sing our songs of praise!
May joy be shining brightly
Within it all our days!

Tho' death may seek to sever
Our golden links of love,
O, may we meet forever
In yonder home above!

Home, home; sweet, sweet home!
God bless our home forever,
Sweet heav'n is mirrored there!

HARRISON MILLARD
"God Bless Our Home Forever" (1872)

Introduction

A Gospel Book for Parents

I WANT TO BE SURROUNDED by little admirers. I wish my kids woke up every day grateful that I am their dad, even proud of me. I wish I went to bed every night with a smile on my face, reflecting on how I had added one more stone to the ever-expanding castle of my parental triumphs. I want to be a brilliant father and an admirable husband more than I want just about anything. With all that commendable desire built up in my heart, it is awfully frustrating that I'm the recurring source of problems in my own house.

Both my activity and passivity, my absence and my presence, can frustrate my family, and that frustrates me even more. I have all the good intentions I can handle, but I stall out with the follow-through. I sit near my kids, wishing I knew how to better engage them, and then when they try to engage me, I struggle to give them the full attention they are looking for. I even fly by the seat of my pants on spiritual leadership. I need help. But sadly, the wisdom I find that should be helpful often fosters even more discouragement. Even the best-intentioned advice can get on my nerves, as it makes me fixate on my blunders. The pursuit of getting better leaves me feeling worse.

There are an astonishing number of books about how to be a better parent. Odds are you've probably read some of them. I'm sure that a lot of what's out there is fantastic and filled with helpful insights. Sometimes when we get stuck, we need books that tell us how and why to do this and how and why not to do that—law books for parents, so to speak.

But this is not a how-to parenting book. It doesn't clash with most of those that are, but it is different. It is far more gospel than law. I am not a perfect dad, and I'm not a clinician with a PhD, ready to solve all your challenges with clever new methods.[1] What I am is a fellow parent and Christ follower, a father and a pastor with a lot to say to discouraged parents. I see them all the time, and I am no stranger to my own personal brand of downheartedness. I'm an empathizing fellow sufferer who has found great relief in the arms of God, and I know so many parents who are starving for that same comfort.

You probably know what it's like to read a how-to parenting book because you want to improve, and sadly, instead of finishing a book feeling encouraged and empowered, you feel as if the bar got even higher, the job got even harder, and you are an even bigger disappointment than you thought. Finishing some books can leave you feeling as if you need more help than when you started. How do you balance all these systems, liturgies, strategies, and new techniques? Someone is trying to offer you wisdom, but all you see is your mistakes, and all you hear is accusatory criticism. The more you take in and the more you understand, the worse off you seemingly are. I've been there too. I know how that feels.

Some of the parents who picked up the book I cowrote with Matt Chandler, *Family Discipleship* (Crossway, 2020), read it and felt inspired and equipped to make disciples in their home, which was the whole

---

1 All the issues we discuss in this book are addressed from a scriptural and pastoral perspective. I believe that this can be beneficial to any reader, especially to those who trust in Christ. I recognize, however, that many of the issues discussed in this book may touch on a matter that is so chronic or significant for the reader that it would be best for that individual to consult a counselor or doctor as well as his or her local pastor. Please receive the words of this book in the spirit in which they were written—from a pastor and fellow stumbling sinner who wants to bless you with God's grace, not a clinician trying to diagnose you from afar or a cynic trying to undermine your medical professional's plan of care.

goal of writing it. But others who read it walked away feeling only more like a failure. And I felt burdened to make sure that parents also hear clearly how the gospel of grace fits with the duty of discipleship.

I wanted to write this book so that I could offer you something unconventional in a parenting book—something I believe parents need desperately. Something that will help you be able to hear what it takes to honor God while attempting to be a great parent and not feel overwhelmed by it. We will miss out on so much if we are so anxious, so stressed, or so discouraged that we can't receive guidance without feeling more lost.

As I said, this is not a how-to resource for you. It's a "how God" book. How God sets you free. How God relieves your burdens. How God grows your faith. How God offers you peace. How God casts off what so easily entangles. How God made a way for you to be fully forgiven for your shortcomings and empowers you for what he has called you to do in your home. You don't need just a list of more *recommendations*. I want to offer you some *relief*.

Don't Eat Dirt, and Don't Waste the Grace

I want to show you how our God blesses parents with faith. He gives rest to exhausted parents. He forgives sinful parents. He comforts afflicted parents. He loves rejected parents. Our God humbles proud parents. He restores failed parents. He is near to brokenhearted parents. Our God is a refuge to desperate parents.

This book is for all the parents who mess up—for those who are wrestling with regrets. This is for the self-torturing perfectionist and the self-justifying slacker, the self-deprecating mother and the self-righteous father. It's for the mom who worries and the dad who fears. This is for the ones who can't find joy because they're too busy dreading the endless list of what-ifs and hypothetical worst-case scenarios. This is a book for the overwhelmed—for the family that wants to be better, do better, and feel better. In other words, this book is for you, and this book is for me.

There are a lot of books that offer us advice. That's great. We need it. But when you keep pumping your mind full of suggestions and yet keep messing up, it can be demoralizing. In addition to more counsel, we could all use some more comfort. I can testify that as a father, I need the thrill of grace as much as I need the benefit of guidance. I could teach you some parenting tips, but what good are they if your heart is not secure in Christ? We could teach your kids to obey, but what good is it ultimately if your heart and their heart don't belong to God? With Jesus and because of Jesus, I want you to be able to hear parenting wisdom and have your confidence reinforced, not shattered. In short, I am writing to you about the grace of God in the gospel so that you can experience how Jesus sets parents free.

Yes, the gospel certainly applies to our soul's freedom from damnation, but that's not all. Believing that God is for you and not against you affects every aspect of your everyday life, not just life after death.

If the hardship you face is because of a diagnosis, a defiant child, a stressful work situation, fatigue, or someone else's sin—really for whatever reason you are facing challenges—our God's gentle heart and his burden-lifting help provide the relief that your family needs. Psalm 34:19 says, "Many are the afflictions of the righteous, but the LORD delivers him out of them all." There is nothing that our God cannot comfort you in and lead you through.

With Christ, your home can be marked less and less by shame, exhaustion, despair, and anxiety, and because you walk in step with the Spirit, it can be marked more and more by gospel fruit like freedom, love, joy, peace, patience, kindness, goodness, faithfulness, gentleness, and self-control. The fruit of the Spirit brings relief to a parent in need. Thus, the rest of what you read in this book is organized around this beautiful fruit.

I am not writing to manipulate you into feeling better about yourself. I actually want to help you get stronger. On this side of heaven, the fruit of the Spirit may not *eliminate* all your shame, anxiety, despair, or exhaustion, but in Christ, it will *alleviate* it. That is my goal in writing to you—to relieve your pain, torment, challenges, and struggles. Until Christ takes all of it away, let us seek the present relief available in the power of God.

As parents, we have tried to find relief in so many deficient sources. Coping with our challenges without Christ is like eating dirt to alleviate hunger—you may stave off your growling stomach, but you have not found a remedy to what's killing you. So many of us are starving for relief, but for some reason we have not turned to the true source of relief in a way that actually helps.

Christian parents, if I may be so bold, allow me to reintroduce you to the profound grace of God. I know you need it. You know you need it. This grace will embolden and encourage you. It will breathe life into you and into the way you lead your home.

A Dangerous Book

A book about freedom and forgiveness can be dangerous. People love to use grace as permission to keep sinning. With so much bad parenting in this world, how can we dare speak to parents of grace and not fear that it will lead to rationalizing or excusing sin in their homes?

Before we jump into these grace-filled chapters, let's make sure we are on the same page about sin. I want to be abundantly clear: Grace is not about taking sin lightly or looking down on God's law. It has nothing to do with condoning or minimizing immorality. In fact, it is the severity and seriousness of sin that makes grace so great. If sin were not so serious, then God's grace would be of little consequence. It is the very severity of our depravity that makes God's mercy so spectacular.

Grace is a gift to us in Christ, but obedience to God is not irrelevant. God's guidance is a gift to us too, and because we love and trust him, we lament disobedience. We have a godly grief. Grace, mercy, and freedom do not mean that sin won't grieve us as parents. There are godly ways we mourn our kids' sins as well as our own. Just like our kids, we lie, we take, we covet, we idolize, and so much more. While self-deprecation and abasement are never a godly response to our sins, it is right to confess our guilt and to feel righteous remorse. Such godly grief is a hurt we experience not because we pity ourselves over the consequences we face but because we have broken God's law, and "godly grief produces a repentance that leads to salvation without regret" (2 Cor. 7:10).

Parents will judge themselves and others about many things that are not sin, but if what we are witnessing in ourselves or others dishonors God, it should be handled appropriately, with gentleness and a desire for restoration.

First, we should review what happened when a mistake is made. You can do this with someone else or on your own. Compare your mistake to what God has commanded. If what happened is not sin but, for whatever reason, is foolish or regrettable, then commit to rejecting any belittling accusations and remember your identity as a child of God, forgiven and free. Missteps cannot get a grip on you that God can't release you from. Ask God to help you grow in wisdom and in maturity but not carry around undue condemnation for yourself.

Second, if what happened was truly wrong, actually sinful, then take responsibility for what you did and repent. Own everything you can. Confess it to God and to the person you sinned against. Do not conceal any of it.

Third, show genuine remorse. There is no condemnation for you in Christ, but there should be conviction to change as well as grief over sin. Yet if you don't feel a sense of sincere remorse, do not fake it. Confess that as well. Pray that the Lord would help you grieve your sin.

Fourth, fully accept all the repercussions of your actions. Being forgiven does not mean that your sin won't have consequences.

Last, remind yourself that you are set free. Your sins are forgiven, and your victory in Christ is secure. Your soul is moored to Jesus.

The only solution to our sin is the grace and mercy of God. Getting grace means receiving blessings that we do not deserve, and getting mercy means not receiving the just punishment for our sin. Grace and mercy are not given because we are not guilty. Whether we are sinners and thus also broken as parents is not up for debate. We need forgiveness. And God is gracious and merciful toward his people! Psalm 103:10–13 says,

> He does not deal with us according to our sins,
>   nor repay us according to our iniquities.
> For as high as the heavens are above the earth,
>   so great is his steadfast love toward those who fear him;
> as far as the east is from the west,
>   so far does he remove our transgressions from us.
> As a father shows compassion to his children,
>   so the LORD shows compassion to those who fear him.

If you can show compassion to your kids, how much more will your perfect heavenly Father be able to show compassion toward you? It's this mercy and compassion that sets us parents free. I love that the Bible uses the family as a metaphor for God's gracious relationship with us. I want your family and the way you feel about it to be a beautiful model of the gospel. I hope that everywhere you turn in your home, you will be constantly reminded of the grace of God.

Kind are the words that Jesus speaks
To cheer the drooping saint;
"My grace sufficient is for you,
Though nature's powers may faint."

"My grace its glories shall display,
And make your griefs remove:
Your weakness shall the triumphs tell
Of boundless power and love."

What though my griefs are not removed,
Yet why should I despair?
While my kind Saviour's arms support,
I can the burden bear.

Jesus, my Saviour and my Lord,
'Tis good to trust Thy name;
Thy power, Thy faithfulness, and love,
Will ever be the same.

Weak as I am, yet through Thy grace
I all things can perform;
And, smiling, triumph in Thy name,
Amid the raging storm.

JOHN NEEDHAM
"My Grace Is Sufficient for Thee" (1792)

1

Important and Impossible

Being a Good Parent

BEING A GREAT PARENT is pretty simple. Good parents always stay involved in their kid's life. At the same time, they never get overinvolved in their kid's life. All it takes to be a great mom or dad is to never overreact and never underreact. Protect your kids from the things in this world that would harm them, but don't overprotect them; otherwise, they won't know how to live independently. Be helpful and serve your kids, but know when to not solve their problems for them. Let them make their own choices but only about some things and gradually, not right away and not always, and sometimes stop them if they make the wrong choice, and sometimes don't stop them so they can experience the natural consequences. Teach them to be kind but not a pushover. Encourage your kids, but don't flatter them. It is great to delight them, but don't spoil them with delights. Provide for them by working, but be home with them, giving them your best energy and attention. Be stern but not scary. Be friendly, but remain a parent and not a buddy. Love your kids with your whole heart but not more than you love God. Don't forget to make the right choices about education, diet, extracurriculars, housing, and socializing, and make sure you teach them about the Bible and Jesus because if you don't, even if you get everything else just right, they will lose it all. Be cautious not to do anything excessively or insufficiently, and remember that the stakes when raising a human are incredibly high. That's parenting. That's not all there is to it, but it's a good start.

The tips and tricks for becoming a good parent form a minefield that is comically frustrating to navigate. They are a never-ending list of straightforward yet urgent and seemingly unattainable, almost contradictory principles. It's avoiding too much of this while not doing too little of that at the same time. It's like teetering on a tightrope while carrying two struggling toddlers. The slightest overreaction or underreaction, and we will fail. Again. It's simple: Parenting is important and impossible.

I Might Be the Villain

When my kids were little, one of them asked us if we could get a piñata for Christmas morning. "Of course!" I thought. "The traditional Christmas-morning piñata!"

I loved the idea. We bought a Darth Vader piñata and some plastic light sabers to smash it with. (For the uninitiated, Darth Vader is the infamous villain in *Star Wars*.) It seemed wonderfully appropriate to be smashing an evil villain to celebrate the incarnation. Everyone loves to see a bad guy lose and good triumph over evil. A great story should always have a compelling villain, and the Christmas story has some all-time greats—namely, King Herod and, cosmically, Satan.

As a pastor, I've had the privilege of hearing many people's personal stories, and in these narratives, the bad guy is usually a parent. In so many of the stories I've heard, at some point at least, Mom or Dad is the antagonist or, if not the antagonist, at least the scapegoat.

We are all largely shaped, for better or worse, by our family of origin. It's one thing to reflect on that personally, but it's a whole new level of intimidation to consider it now as a parent yourself. We need a word more emphatic than "daunting" to describe the feeling of knowing that our parenting is informing and shaping another person's story and that we might be the story's villain. (I hope there's not some future Christmas morning when my kids are therapeutically smashing a dad piñata.)

I know that most of what I do with my life won't have a huge impact, but my parenting, at the same time, for better or worse, can reverberate for generations. This work really matters, and I want to do it right, so I am always thinking about how to do it better. It's incredibly important.

Yet it has crossed my mind many times that I might one day be the bad guy in part of my sons' stories, that I'll be the one they must overcome. But so help me God, I don't want that for our family. I don't want to be the villain in my kids' lives. I don't want to be their opponent.

We can all find faults in our parents. Who can see parents' failings better or be more directly affected by them than their own kids? I feel the pain my sin causes, and so do my children. I can already see how my mistakes have a ripple effect on their lives. Add to that the fact that they will often resist my best efforts and intentions, and it's no wonder that parenting is so incredibly hard. It grieves me that I'm not doing better. I want to parent exactly right. But that is, unfortunately, impossible.

Parenthood is both very important and impossible to get exactly right, an intimidating combination. Important and impossible. It's no wonder that parenting brings with it bouts of shame, pressure, despair, anxiety, and exhaustion. Putting everything we've got into the pursuit of the important and the impossible will inevitably lead to trials, disappointments, and failures. It's literally overwhelming.

So praise God that he does not leave us to our own devices. If we had only our own strength to rely on, if we were not empowered by the Holy Spirit, if there was no grace for us, or if we could not be helped in our labors by God, we would not be more than conquerors—we'd be less than losers. Our households would be hopeless.

Shalak It All

Right now, my family is at a stage when our youngest son has so much confidence in my love for him that if he finds me sitting on the couch, he will, with a running start, leap onto me and expect to be welcomed onto my lap with open arms. He will jump onto me, uninvited, and fully expect to be embraced and delighted in. Sometimes I don't even see him coming. He has faith that my love for him is so secure that he doesn't need to ask. He trusts that I'll catch him. He trusts that I want him close. He trusts that he's safe with me. He assumes he is wanted. And he is not wrong. In fact, my love for him is so sincere and so substantial and so steadfast that I can't imagine there will ever be a day when I wouldn't delight to embrace him and protect him. When he comes close to me now, we cling to each other, not out of fear but out of genuine love. We delight to be by each other.

The remedy for so many of our struggles as parents is found in having faith that we can jump into the arms of God and be welcomed and protected. We can cling to God out of genuine love for one another, God for us and us for God. Assuming we are wanted by God changes our entire outlook on life. If I, an imperfect father, can so thoroughly delight in embracing and protecting my child, how much more sincere, substantial, and steadfast must the love of our perfect heavenly Father be for us?

Jesus prays for you in John 17, and in that prayer, we glimpse his description of the Father's love. In verse 23, Jesus prays to the Father, "The glory that you have given me I have given to them, . . . that the world may know that you sent me and loved them even as you loved me." What if you genuinely believed that God the Father feels about you the way he feels about Jesus Christ? How welcome are you in his presence? How cherished are you?

There is relief for every struggle found in knowing and believing that we are safe with God and that God wants us close. Jesus says, "Come to me," and what the Lord says, he means (Matt. 11:28). He will catch us. He embraces us with compassion like a loving father (Luke 15). He comforts us. As we have faith that God delights in us, we, like sheep with a good shepherd, will not be in want (Ps. 23).

He can even cultivate our trust in his love and restore us after our mistakes. Just look at Peter in Luke 5 and John 21. Soon after Peter first meets Jesus, he sees Jesus make the first miraculous catch of fish. After witnessing the power of Christ, Peter drops to his knees and tells Jesus to get away from him. He wants Jesus to go away because he sees himself as a very sinful man and therefore assumes he will be unwanted. This is the voice of shame. Humans crumble under the weight of their inabilities and transgressions. They want to hide.

But Jesus does not oblige Peter's request. He does not go away. He actually tells Peter to let go of his fears. Then they spend the next three years in close proximity to one another, and after three years of developing this relationship, Peter reacts quite differently when he sees Jesus perform a similar miracle a second time.

This event occurs soon after Peter makes his most notorious mistake—publicly denying Jesus multiple times not long after swearing he would never abandon Jesus. Yet even after this significant misstep, Jesus reveals himself to the disciples after his crucifixion by helping them catch fish, and Peter no longer wants Jesus to go away. Peter has changed. His fear is gone. He trusts the love of Jesus for him now, even considering his own sin. Peter can't wait to be close to Jesus. Since he is in the boat with the miraculous catch and Jesus is on the shore a hundred yards away, he dives into the water to get to Jesus as soon as possible. Peter is no less sinful than when he and Jesus first met, but even in his sin, he now assumes that he is wanted and welcomed by God. He trusts Jesus. He has faith that he will be comforted and secure with Christ.

Peter is not wrong. Jesus does not condemn and reject Peter when he comes to him. Jesus restores him. They walk with each other, and that bears fruit in Peter's life.

When we walk with God, Paul tells us, it will produce certain outcomes in our lives. In Galatians 5, Paul describes this as "fruit." He lists the results of walking with God as love, joy, peace, patience, kindness, goodness, faithfulness, gentleness, and self-control. It's this fruit that is such a relief to the heart of a Christian parent.

Such fruit, says Paul, attests to our freedom in Christ as well. Freedom is one of Christianity's most basic and beautiful doctrines. Christians are freed from serving sin as master so that they can follow a better master. In Galatians 5:1, Paul says, "For freedom Christ has set us free." In John 8:31–32, Jesus states, "If you abide in my word, you are truly my disciples, and you will know the truth, and the truth will set you free." And just a few verses later, he says, "If the Son sets you free, you will be free indeed" (8:36). This book is all about that freedom and how it affects our parenting.

By grace through faith, Christians get released from the consequences of their sin. The sacrifice of Christ has satisfied every one of our debts. We are freed from the penalty of breaking God's law, and we are set free from the evil that would ravage us if we didn't live according to God's limits with God as our Master. We are free from trying to earn our righteousness. Now we can serve God and each other, free of the fear of condemnation for our imperfections and trusting in the goodness of his commands.

While Christians are not freed from facing trouble, we are freed from hopelessness and despair. Jesus says that even in tribulation we can "take heart" because he has already overcome the world (John 16:33). That same Peter who races to see Christ after his worst public mistakes reminds us that we can cast all our burdens on God. As a Christian parent, you get to cast "all your anxieties on him, because he cares for you" (1 Pet. 5:7). Did you hear that? *All* your anxieties. *All* your burdens. *All* your worries. Because he cares for you, everything that weighs you down can be cast from you to him.

In this passage, Peter is quoting Psalm 55:22, "Cast your burden on the LORD, and he will sustain you." The Hebrew word for "cast" here is *shalak*. It means to throw, hurl, or chuck something. It's a great word. Imagine getting to ball up all your anxiety, bitterness, exhaustion, frustration, shame, and stress into a massive ugly ball of weighty negativity and then getting to *shalak* it! Chuck it all off a cliff. You can take the burdens and pressures that are weighing on you and hurl them down. When you don't feel strong enough to even lift them, you have permission just to drop them. You are invited to fling your burdens at the feet of God. Your God wants to unburden you. Instead of holding on to all that mess, you get to throw it off.

And that's not all. Regarding all those struggles, you aren't only unburdened but also offered a gift in exchange. If you cast off anxiety and cling to the Prince of Peace like a beloved child clings to his mother, you will receive peace in your life. If you chuck your bitterness and cling to the kindness of God, you will grow in kindness. If you hurl down all the undue stresses you feel and cling to the God who loves you, you will grow love in your heart. If you let go of all your inadequacy and cling to the goodness of God, you will become good yourself. What an exchange! Now that is serious freedom.

The Home-Free Home

I believe that Christian parents would feel much freer and even more confident about their roles at home if they could just be convinced to operate out of the assumption that they are now and forever home-free. The term *home-free* refers to the profound relief, elation, and liberation that comes from knowing that nothing can defeat you. It's the presumption of invincibility that comes from being convinced that nobody can come between you and your finish line. The race is already won. Your success is certain.

Being home-free does not necessarily mean being completely done or finished with your work. There might still be some difficult tasks ahead, even some things you don't want to do. What it means is that there is nothing left that is strong enough to take your victory away from you. Triumph is a guaranteed result.

Sailors on a ship that has been violently tossed by the waves of the open sea in a storm desperately hope for deliverance and a sense of security that comes only when they have finally made it into the protected safety of a harbor. They are not yet on the shore, but they've cleared the danger. They are home-free. There's a final dash in an ob-stacle course when the runner has hurdled the last barrier or turned the last corner and there's nothing between her and the finish line except a flat straightaway. She's home-free. There's a point on an oak tree that a squirrel can scurry up to where it is out of reach of any sprinting, leap-ing dog. Escape to that height, and the squirrel is home-free. There's a depth a fish can plunge to where a diving eagle can't snatch it. Make it to that depth, and the fish is home-free. Knowing you're home-free is knowing you can't lose.

For the Christian, being home-free is the relief, elation, and freedom that comes after hearing and trusting the gospel. It's the result of having faith that we are safe in the arms of God. It's an invincible contentment that comes from believing the promises of God for those who trust in Christ. For Christians, being home-free is the absolute assurance we possess that Christ died for us and that because of his finished work on the cross, his resurrection from the dead, and the salvation extended to those who trust in him, we are forgiven, justified, and cleansed from all unrighteousness. We are secure. Fortified. Cherished. Home-free.

If you are a Christian, you have been home-free since the moment you joined the family of God, and you will be home-free forever because of it. As you exhaled your last breath as an unsaved soul and took your first breath as a saint, you were irrevocably liberated. Born again. Home-free.

You have also been gifted with a sacred book—a book of truths and promises regarding your malady, your liberator, and even your future. The Bible was written by the one who knows and shapes your destiny, and he has been generous enough to reveal your fate to you. He has declared it, and he determines it. You get the privilege of living your life as someone who already knows your story's ending. The worst thing that could happen to you *will not happen*, and the best thing that could ever happen to you is totally guaranteed. Though suffering may not be less common or less painful for you, though you will still face temptation and sin in this life, truly nothing can prevent you from reaching your ultimate destination. You live content and at peace, persevering in affliction, because you are home-free.

Oh, what joy fills the heart of the parent who is home-free and knows it! It is a transcendent relief. Even death has lost its sting. Nothing can take away the victory and love that the Christ follower has been given in Jesus. This is the victory we so eagerly invite our kids to see and plead with God to grant to our whole household. There's no greater blessing for the Christian parent than to see the seeds of gospel truth we plant grow, by God, into a victorious faith in our children.

Home-free, however, is not the same thing as hurt-free. Jesus was perfect, but even he got hurt. Jesus got sad. Jesus did everything right and was still rejected—often. But when he was hurting, he still had peace. His love did not waver. His joy was consistent. His patience did not run out. He got hurt but stayed faithful. He was persistently gentle.

Because of Jesus, your victory is assured, but you can still expect to be hurt. What I want to help you see is a path not to a hurt-free home but to a home-free home. Jesus got hurt, but he was never anxious, never hopeless, never ashamed, and never bitter. Walking with Jesus will lead you into more of that freedom. The home-free family can bounce back from anything knowing that God's mercies are new every morning. The home-free family can face any hardship or difficulty knowing that God works all things together for good for the sake of those who love him.

Christian parents, I assume that many of you already know this. Most of you would agree with every statement I just made. So, then, these questions must be asked: Why is it so easy for us to parent as if we *don't* believe it? Why do we parent our kids stressed and scrambling, as if we don't know who will win? Why do we parent with so much shame when we are cherished, forgiven, and free? Why do we fret so much when we know God can be trusted? Why do we exhaust ourselves by parenting out of our own strength instead of being renewed in the Spirit? Why do we parent in a panic, as though our children's salvation is something we can secure if our efforts are intense enough?

I want us to parent as people who are genuinely convinced that because of the grace of God, we are home-free. We are running in a race that has already been won. Until we enter the final joy of our Master, let's "lay aside every weight, and sin which clings so closely, and let us run with endurance the race that is set before us, looking to Jesus, the founder and perfecter of our faith" (Heb. 12:1–2).

That gospel truth should bring you relief. I believe that the fruit of the Spirit will alleviate or even deliver you from what discourages your heart and your mind as you parent.

Relief is a wonderful feeling. It's like sitting down after you've stood so long that your feet ache from bearing the weight. That's relief. It's like finding comfortable shade on a sweltering, sunny day. That's relief. It's like chugging water when your throat is parched. That's relief. This is the kind of feeling we can get in our parenting if we rely on God through faith.

When you're not hungry, eating food can be a nice experience. But when you are starving, when your stomach is growling and it has been too long since your last meal, food tastes different. When you feel real hunger, the first morsel is an almost overwhelming delight. Every sense is engaged, your tastebuds are hypersensitive, and your whole body is ministered to as you chew your first bite. It's like a breath of air after being underwater for too long. I hope that's what reading these gospel truths is like for you. I hope that your hungry, anxious, stressed, bitter soul is satisfied in the gospel of Jesus Christ and that your whole family is ministered to by these words.

Experience the Exchange

The physical body that God designed for you does some incredible things. One of them is that you are constantly exchanging the gases you don't need for the ones that keep you alive. You are breathing in oxygen and breathing out carbon dioxide. The process of breathing in is called "inspiration" and breathing out "expiration." You do this all day unconsciously.

What I want you to do right now is to slow down for a minute and consider the process more intentionally. Consciously breathe in slowly. Intentionally breathe out slowly and deeply. Think about this exchange and how it illustrates the exchange that I am discussing in this chapter. Breathe out slowly as you imagine casting away all your shame. Breathe in slowly, thinking about how you receive and cling to freedom. Breathe out slowly, thinking about casting off your anxiety. Breathe in slowly, thinking about receiving the peace of God. As your body expels what you don't need and takes in what you do, imagine how God encourages you to get rid of your burdens and cultivate the fruit that comes from walking with him.

As you breathe in slowly, consider what it would feel like to cling to God like a beloved child. As you breathe out slowly, consider what it would feel like to ball up all your struggles, chuck them, and walk away from them. As you breathe in, consider the mistakes you've made. As you breathe out, consider the grace and mercy of God given to you. After taking a few moments to breathe, pray.

A Prayer for Casting and Clinging

Heavenly Father, I confess that I have not been a model parent. My children see things in me that I wish they didn't. Sometimes I am overwhelmed by the weight of the tasks you've assigned me. I am weighed down by how much there is to do and how much it takes out of me to do it. In my pursuit of being better, I often feel worse.

I want to surrender all these burdens to you. Help me drop what I've been carrying. Take it off my shoulders when I don't have the strength to cast it away. Give me the courage to ask for help. Please whisper peace to my restless heart. Remind me of my victory in your Son Jesus Christ. Help me loosen my grip on my struggles and cling to you instead. Make me stronger when my home requires strength. Make me wiser when my family needs wisdom. Give me faith when I'm tempted to crumble.

Where I've been timid and weary, make me confident. Let me be overcome by a sense of sincere relief. I want to know your freedom, and I want to live unbound, unburdened, and set free as a parent. Amen.

Reflection Questions

1. What is something from this chapter that stuck out to you?

2. When it comes to parenting, what feels important to you right now?

3. What feels impossible to get right lately?

4. How would you describe your parenting struggles at the moment? What burdens would you like to *shalak*, to cast off?

5. What would you like to see change in your home? What role do you think God might have you play in changing it?

6. What would you like to see change in your heart toward your family?

Lord, we confess our numerous faults,
How great our guilt has been!
Foolish and vain were all our thoughts,
And all our lives were sin.

But, O my soul! for ever praise,
For ever love His name,
Who turns thy feet from dangerous ways
Of folly, sin, and shame.

'Tis not by works of righteousness
Which our own hands have done;
But we are saved by sovereign grace
Abounding through His Son.

'Tis from the mercy of our God
That all our hopes begin;
'Tis by the water and the blood
Our souls are wash'd from sin.

'Tis through the purchase of His death
Who hung upon the tree,
The Spirit is sent down to breathe
On such dry bones as we.

Raised from the dead, we live anew;
And, justified by grace,
We shall appear in glory too,
And see our Father's face.

ISAAC WATTS
"Salvation by Grace" (1709)

2

Freedom

Relief from Shame

IMAGINE THAT YOU MADE a parenting mistake. A bad one. Again. And it haunts you. Your inner voice begins to ramble about all your latest shortcomings. It is an onslaught of self-condemnation and self-torment. *Why did you say what you said? To your own child! Why did you do what you did? You are supposed to be the adult who knows better, who sets the example! Think of the damage you might have done and the mess you made for yourself. What are you going to do now? You should be ashamed.* You judge, and you judge, and you judge, and you find yourself lacking. You did too much of this. You didn't do enough of that.

Now imagine that you have some critical thoughts about other parents. You begin to consider some other families that you know and how they are different from you. They are a mess. Dysfunctional. (*So are you, but not like that.*) You hear how they speak to each other. You wouldn't have said it like that. That family is giving too much freedom to their kids. This family is smothering their children. That family is too harsh. This family is overcommitted. That family is lazy. This family is too rich (*must be nice*). Those kids are spoiled. These kids are rude. Those kids need discipline. These kids need love. Those families should be ashamed. You judge, and you judge, and you judge, and you find these families lacking. Those families are doing too much of this. These families are not doing enough of that.

In the wake of mistakes, many of our hearts default to shame and to shaming others. But if you scour the Scriptures, you will not find "shame" on the list of fruits of the Spirit. Cruel shame is not a gift from God to his people. Any and all shame can be relieved by the freedom we have in Christ.

Impaired Judgment

To be completely honest with you, I love being a father, but parenting has been a constant source of criticism in my heart, both toward myself and others. It's second nature to me to be hard on myself when I mess up as a dad, and it comes naturally to me to criticize the parenting of others around me.

If you don't think there is an inner critic in you, I dare you to sit on the sideline of some youth sports game or walk around a theme park and see how long you can go before you start to instinctively evaluate others. A few years ago, my family and I went to a theme park together, and everywhere I looked there were either families who I thought were having more fun than us (how dare they!) or families being rude to each other in ways we'd never tolerate. As kids cried and yanked on their parent's arms while waiting to meet costumed cartoon characters, I saw husbands and wives shooting each other looks that could kill and swapping enraged whispers (that made me feel sad for them and grossly better about myself at the same time). The thoughts I was having revealed that there was something wrong going on in my heart.

Parenting is a challenge for everyone. There are always ways to do better, and because of that, all of us wrestle with some tangle of shame and shaming others. I opened this chapter with some examples of that. I need you to see, however, that shame is not our root issue. As common as shame is for parents, it is the fruit of a more insidious problem. The guilt you experience and any disdain you have for (or receive from) other families both stem from the same dangerous reality you may not have considered: You have a judgment problem.

Parenting shame comes from an inward-looking self-judgment that assesses situations with a biased and often unkind perspective. Parenting pride develops out of a prejudiced and often merciless appraisal of others. Our inability to be impartial, our inadequate wisdom, our finite knowledge, and our modest capacity for compassion and mercy make us unreliable and undesirable judges. The judgments levied in your heart toward yourself and others are coming from an unqualified judge—you. Human judgment is impaired. The reason we have a judgment problem is that *we* are acting as judges. It's a personnel issue. You have a judgment problem because you have a judge problem.

Yes, there are some scriptures that refer to times when believers will act as judges in the future, but I can assure you that those verses are not referring to the kind of harsh, shaming, and condemning judgments that are so common in the belittling, negative critiques we typically direct toward ourselves and others. Further, there are many scriptures that warn us about the dangers of presuming to sit in judgment. I promise you that we do not have permission from God to replace him as Judge.

Consider James 4:12, which says, "There is only one lawgiver and judge, he who is able to save and to destroy. But who are you to judge your neighbor?" There is just one true Judge, and as you'll see, that's actually very good news. Unlike you, the true Judge has the power to condemn *and* the power to rescue. And if you are in Christ Jesus, the Judge delights in you. He is merciful and kind, and his love is steadfast. He is your judge and liberator, your exonerator and emancipator.

A Honey Badger Tongue

One of my sons is great at asking people thoughtful questions and posing interesting hypotheticals. One of his classics is "If you could tame any wild animal and have it for a bodyguard, what would you choose?"

My boys are in a lion and wolf cub phase (high cuteness factor), but I believe the best answer is a honey badger. Honey badgers will fight lions, hyenas, venomous snakes, and bees and are tenacious even when they are outnumbered. One cuddly honey badger for me, please!

In James 3:7–10, the apostle says that the tongue is like an animal that no one can tame. Basically, James is saying that it is easier to wrestle a ferocious honey badger into submission than to lock down what you say and how you judge. He points out that the same tongue we use to praise God is used to insult people who bear God's image. Aloud and in our mind, we insult the parent on the opposing sports team who screams, the kid who bothers us, and the person we see in the mirror—we are insult factories. According to James, this "ought not to be so" (3:10). That's a polite early-church way of saying, "This is not okay! Stop it!" That might be the best biblical advice anyone could give you on shame. Shame would start to dissolve if you could stop insulting God's image bearers (including you).

The severe, scornful words that you say to yourself, words that shame and abuse, dear brother or sister, are not the words that Jesus uses for you. His heart is gentle. Do you think he doesn't know your failures better than you do? Do you think they are insurmountable for him? Listen to God's words for you: "For whenever our heart condemns us, God is greater than our heart, and he knows everything" (1 John 3:20). God is greater than our condemning hearts.

The demeaning, insulting words that you use for other families or for your spouse are not the things that Christ has for them and certainly not something he delights to hear from you. Let those go. Cast those words down. Every person is made in the image of God and endowed with inherent dignity. There is no true comfort in finding yourself more acceptable than others. You are free from the need to compare, covet, and condescend. The failures of others do not absolve you of your sins, and the successes of others should not discourage you, "for you were called to freedom, brothers. Only do not use your freedom as an opportunity for the flesh, but through love serve one another"

(Gal. 5:13). God has set you free and called you to love and serve others, not sneer at them or be stepped on by them.

Hiding and Blaming

When one of my sons was very young and new to toilet training, like many of us in that trying season, he had an accident. At first, he claimed that it wasn't him that did it. The evidence didn't seem to back him up, but he swore he did not wet his pants. Not to call my son a liar, but if there really was another culprit, they did the best job of framing someone that I have ever seen—the perfect crime, you might say. And if my son was innocent, then the real criminal is still at large. He got away with it, and he's probably out there somewhere right now hatching his next nefarious plot to soil someone's jeans.

Shame makes us want to hide and blame. Since the garden of Eden, when people mess up, they have wanted the false relief that comes from hiding their sin where no one will find it or pointing their finger at someone else to transfer the guilt. The gift of freedom in Christ is a true relief, one without any need to shift responsibility or cover up what happened. It's merciful, full liberation. While we were still guilty, our God took the full weight of our mistakes on himself without pretending as if they didn't happen.

As for judgment, because you are united to Christ, you are free from the pressure of living your life according to the appraisal and expectations of anyone other than God. The only verdict that matters is his. Paul says in 1 Corinthians 4:3–4, "It is a very small thing that I should be judged by you or by any human court. In fact, I do not even judge myself. . . . It is the Lord who judges me." You are free from the condemnation that comes from other people. You're free from self-condemnation. The measure of your worth rests solely in God.

Being free from human judgments does not mean, however, that advice is irrelevant to you. Being free means you should be able to hear and receive godly wisdom from someone without falling prey to a sense of condemnation. God often uses the people around us to help us follow him. Much like our children, every parent needs wisdom and gentle correction. We all have lessons left to learn. In Christ, we are free enough to listen to the opinions of others without receiving input as an insult. Being truly free in Christ means that even if a stranger makes an unsolicited remark about your parenting, you can hear it without being offended. Anything that needs to be corrected in your family, you'll be happy to receive. You can even be grateful for it. You are so free that anything you don't need to take in can roll right off your back.

I genuinely want to experience that level of freedom from human judgments in my life. I imagine you do too, and yet parents like us seem devoted to a life of trying to be judges. It's truly ludicrous that we *choose* to listen to human judgments over the Lord's.

If you were on trial and got to choose between a judge who was famous for knowing everything there was to know, dealing out incredible mercy, and setting people free by paying their debts for them and a judge who was notorious for jumping to conclusions, humiliating defendants, and being unforgiving, whom would you pick? The gospel is the good news that you and your peers are relieved of judge duty because there is a better Judge—one who is more merciful and compassionate and wiser than you have imagined. Following Jesus means gaining freedom from unreliable and undesirable human judgment.

Confidence Before God

If a child of yours came to you with an unfair judgment about himself, how would you respond? If your son were wallowing in self-pity because of a mistake he made, would you heap more shame on him? If your daughter were beaming with pride because she thought she was smarter than another child, would you humiliate her to deflate her pride?

If you, even in your imperfect parenting, wouldn't do those things to your child, then trust and believe that our perfect God would not humiliate or shame you. You know how to love your child when he is berating himself. How much more does our perfect heavenly Father know what you need when you fail? You know how to love and guide your child when her head is swollen with arrogance. How much better does our perfect Judge know how to forgive you and correct you when you are being self-righteous?

The solution to our heart's judgments is not a better performance or a favorable comparison. Emancipation does not come from minimizing our mistakes or inflating our good qualities. The good news is not that you will stand before our Judge, Jesus Christ, one day and be able to say, "I tried my best!" and that your best will be enough. It is not that you will stand before him and say, "Others were worse than me!" and their behavior will make you seem adequate. The question asked by the better Judge is never "Did you feel humiliated enough about your mistakes?" The question our Judge asks is "Do you trust me?"

If the answer to that question is yes, well then, brothers and sisters, the Bible tells us that we get to walk into the courtroom of our Judge with confidence. Can you even imagine that? Picture it—you walk *confidently* into the throne room of the almighty God. Most of us can't even step in front of a mirror with confidence. How could that level of poise and courage in front of God be possible? Because of the love of Christ, our hearts are so free that we fear nothing in God's presence. We quit trusting our own critical assumptions and turn instead to God's declarations. From him we receive a reliable, desirable verdict and true freedom.

Our confidence as Christian parents is rooted not in our estimation of our own excellence but in the finished work of Christ. That same Jesus who loves you, sacrifices for you, and guides you now sits as your qualified Judge. Like it or not, he sits on the judgment seat. No one else.

And one day you will give him an account of your life, including your parenting. That sounds intimidating, but remember that you will be giving an account to the God who loves you better than you are able to love yourself. His love for you is a result not of the smallness of your sin or of the greatness of your good deeds. What a meager love we would merit if that were the case. But no, God always loves you better than you deserve.

If we could find all that we needed within our own hearts, thoughts, deeds, and families, then Jesus and his gospel of rising from the dead in victory over sin and death would be completely unnecessary. If that were true, the church might as well preach, "Just try your best!" If that were true, then instead of Jesus declaring, "I am with you always, to the end of the age" (Matt. 28:20), he might as well have said, "Well, I'll leave you to it. I'm sure you'll be fine!"

No—you are declared righteous solely because of the work of the righteous Judge on your behalf. Your confidence comes from knowing who you are in Christ. Here is some of the best parenting news you'll ever hear: You are not your judge. Someone better sits in that seat. You are of immeasurable value to the real Judge. The rightful Judge loved you enough to live, die, and rise again so that you could be free. The good news is that when you stand before Christ one day to give an account of your family, you will be able to say, "My worst was horrible, my best wasn't good enough, but Jesus, I fully trust your love for me."

The solution to our heart's judgments starts with relinquishing our grip on the judgment seat. When you catch yourself judging, confess and forsake that judgment, and you will receive mercy from the true Judge. I promise you'll see that there's immense relief in getting to end your career as a judge. There is freedom available for you from the only capable and mighty Judge, who sees you the best and loves you the most. Only through a better Judge, Jesus, are the guilty justified and declared righteous. The one who is in Christ, though as much a sinner as anyone else, is free because of his grace.

Grace for You and from You

How hard is it for you to forgive your children when they sin? Would you enjoy being malicious and cruel to them? Do you love to see them suffer from their mistakes? For parents, it is easy to have compassion on our children, to love them better than they deserve. We want to see them set free from sin and shame. So why is it so hard to extend that same love and grace toward ourselves?

In Matthew 18, Jesus tells a parable about a servant's insurmountable debt. The servant is granted freedom, and his massive debt is forgiven by his master. But then that same forgiven man refuses to forgive his fellow servant a tiny, insignificant debt. This is an important message to us as parents. God has been extremely gracious to you. What he gave to you in Christ, you get to cheerfully give to others. Ephesians 4:32 says, "Be kind to one another, tenderhearted, forgiving one another, as God in Christ forgave you." Whether you are looking at your child, considering another family, or looking in the mirror, you get to be gracious.

Jesus says in Luke 6:36–37, "Be merciful, even as your Father is merciful," and he immediately follows that up with "Judge not, and you will not be judged; condemn not, and you will not be condemned; forgive, and you will be forgiven." As we've already seen, you get to be gracious to others because God has been so exceedingly gracious to you. And you can also be gracious to yourself.

Being gracious to ourselves is a struggle for a lot of parents. For some reason, we often refuse to forgive ourselves even though we believe that God has forgiven us. Instead of accepting God's verdict and then being kind with our inner voice, we whisper offensive things about ourselves that we would never put up with from someone else. We decide to let our self-assessment overrule the assessment of God. This is a demonstration of extreme pride. No one can look at the God who knows everything and be correct in saying, "You're wrong about me!"

There is no benefit to resisting or refusing to believe God's grace. When you deny his mercy for you, you once again try to take the place of God in your own life. But he is not under your authority; you are under his. So look at yourself and say, "God's right about me. I'm free. I'm forgiven. What a relief." Instead of refusing to be free and choosing to cling to your own harsh judgment, accept and receive that "though your sins are like scarlet, they shall be as white as snow" (Isa. 1:18).

God's gospel for parents makes me think of the cast-iron skillet my family has been cooking in for years. It's well seasoned. Food doesn't stick to it. There's no telling how many meals it has prepared for us. In fact, the longer it's used and the more it's cared for, the better it gets. I want our hearts and minds to be like well-seasoned cast iron—the more we go through, the more we understand God's grace, and the more we mature in Christ, the more we will see how the gospel keeps accusations and shame from sticking to us. The things that used to make us feel ashamed and condemned will slide right off.

You can almost hear God interrupting our judgments of ourselves and others to say, "There is therefore now no condemnation for those who are in Christ Jesus" (Rom. 8:1). None. "Who shall bring any charge against God's elect?" (Rom. 8:33). No one. So let's conduct ourselves like people who are not condemned. We have been forgiven an insurmountable debt, and we get to walk away free.

Free to Be Yourself

Even as some of you read this chapter about freedom, the judging voice in your heart is condemning you. If you struggle with shame, you might be thinking you are being chided, that I'm saying, "Don't be like that; be like this! What is wrong with you?"

I'm not telling you to stop being who you are at all. Almost the exact opposite. I'm pleading with you to see yourself for who you *truly* are in Christ. I want you to see the real, relieved, and free you. I'm not trying to scold you into a different perspective; I'm trying to pull back the veil your judgment has put over your eyes and help you believe that you are who God says you are. In Christ, you have an imperishable inheritance. You are home-free.

But free to what? Free to judge for yourself? Free to condemn yourself and others? Free to sin? Free to forsake good works? Free to replace God as Judge? Absolutely not! God's freedom is not permission to make performance and comparison our measure of value, nor is it freedom to pursue disobedience or take God's place from him. That would be part of returning to a "yoke of slavery" (Gal. 5:1).

You have been set free not only *from* something but also *for* something. Christians are saved from sin and death so that they can do good works. God set us free so that now, instead of always running toward sin, judgment, and condemnation, we get to run toward him and the gospel gifts he offers.

There are no restrictions on and no limits to these gifts. There is no such thing as too much love, joy, peace, patience, kindness, goodness, faithfulness, gentleness, and self-control.

If you, like so many, are struggling with shame, the relief you need isn't found in hiding, it's not found in pride, and it's not found in self-improvement. Those are false relief. The relief you need is found in faith. Faith in Jesus Christ, who sets you free. Trust that your Savior Jesus has paid the price of your shame. Shame might grow, but so does faith.

As a follower of Christ, this is what the Judge has for you: He loves you. You are a joy to him. He suffers with and for you. He is gentle with your hurts. He is kind to you. He is generous to you. You have his attention. He forgives you.

In Christ, you are free. Believe that. Let the truth of his goodness and your freedom wash over you. You get to parent home-free, victorious in a way that no one can take away. You are not just exonerated but emancipated.

The good news for you as a parent is not just that you are justified before God, declared righteous despite your guilt. The good news is also that you are set free from sin as your master and from shame as your burden to bear. You are free indeed.

Take a moment right now and stand up. Spread your arms wide. Stretch them as far as they will go. Take as deep a breath as your lungs will allow. Shame does not cling to you. You are unchained. Unbound. Unburdened. Home-free.

A Prayer for Times of Mistake Making and Shame

Heavenly Father, help me see lies of condemnation for what they are. Enable me to believe your declaration of freedom from my head to my toes. Give me a heart of discernment without a critical spirit. Show me how to release my grip from the judgment seat that is rightfully yours. Forgive me for attempting to be the judge instead of trusting you to judge. Forgive me for how I have insulted you by insulting myself and others. Help me tame my tongue. You are righteous in ways that I will never be, and I am blessed by your grace. Protect me from cringing over my past and bracing for my future.

Make me as gracious toward myself and others as you are toward me. Show me how to use your grace and freedom to bless my home. Amen.

Reflection Questions

1. What is something that other parents do that you find yourself harshly judging?

2. Who are the best parents you know? What do you think makes them great?

3. What kinds of things do you say to yourself about your own parenting?

4. Why do you think it is so easy to judge yourself and others?

5. If a stranger made a remark about your parenting, how would you respond?

6. If you were as gracious to yourself and others as God is to you, what would change in your home?

All ye who seek a sure relief
In trouble or distress,
Whatever sorrow vex the mind,
Or guilt the soul oppress;
Jesus, who gave Himself for us
Upon the cross to die,
Unfolds to us His sacred heart;
O, to that heart draw nigh.

Ye hear how kindly He invites,
Ye hear His words so blest:
"All ye that labour come to Me,
And I will give you rest."
O Jesus, joy of saints on high;
Thou hope of sinners here;
Attracted by these loving words,
To Thee I lift my prayer.

Wash Thou my wounds in that dear blood
Which forth from Thee did flow;
New grace, new hope inspire; a new
And better life bestow.
Praise Him who with the Father sits
Enthroned upon the skies;
Whose blood redeems our souls from guilt,
Whose Spirit sanctifies.

EDWARD CASWALL
"All Ye Who Seek a Sure Relief" (1849)

3

Love

Relief from Stress

YOU *HAVE* TO. You have to feed your kids. You have to get up in the middle of the night when they cry. You have to wash their clothes. You have to help them with their homework. You have to remind them over and over again to do the things that you've asked them to do. You have to have hard talks about what it means to grow up. You have to tell them about Jesus. You have to discipline them. You have to get them where they're going, and you have to get them from where they've been. You have to shop for them. You have to work to provide for them. You have to put aside your own life and work to listen to them. You have to get this right. You have to find the time. You *have* to do it all!

You have to because you are supposed to. It's not just an expectation, it's an obligation. You don't want to know what would happen if you didn't do all the things you have to do for your kids.

On the other hand, in a heart set free by love, you get to. You get to feed them. You get to hold them even in the middle of the night. You get to serve them. You get to help them. You get to talk with them. You get to help them grow up. You get to discipline them. You get to tell them about Jesus. You get to be with them where they are going, and you get to talk with them about where they've been. You get to provide for them. You get to put aside anything and everything so that you can listen to them. You get to make the time. You get to do it all.

You get to because you love to. These labors aren't chores; they're a privilege. You don't want to know what it would be like if you didn't get to do all the things you do for your kids. When we are dizzy over our to-do list, it's God's love for us and our love for him that reorients how we see our work and mission.

We've Been Duped

You will not find "overwhelming anxiety" listed as a fruit of the Spirit. Feeling stressed about carrying impossible expectations on your shoulders is not how God describes walking with him. Jesus says that the Pharisees put impossible loads on people's shoulders but that, unlike them, he *lifts* burdens. There is a huge weight of pressure on parents regarding who to be and what to do, but those stresses can be relieved by the love that grows out of walking by the Spirit.

I assume that you have felt the pressure to be a better parent (or even to be a perfect parent). I assume you've felt the pressure to get everything done that your family needs. You've been weighed down by the sheer gravity of the role God gave you. But if you stop and think for a minute about where those overwhelming stresses are coming from, you'll notice that most of the negative pressures you feel are internal. They are coming from you. The stress is related to what you have to do, but the distress you feel about it is coming from you and directed inward. So that's where we'll address it now—in your heart.

It turns out that the love God cultivates in your heart can transform every pressured "have to" into a "get to." We lose sleep. We wipe bottoms. We are inconvenienced. We gladly do things we would not otherwise want to do because we love our children. We gladly do things that lead us into hardship and suffering because we love the God who has called us to do them and because it is our delight to love the little "neighbor[s]" who live in our home as we love ourselves (Mark 12:31).

One of the main causes of parental stress is being tricked into believing that blessings are burdens. If you've been duped into believing that a child is an impediment to your life, then it's no wonder the work of parenting stresses you. When you lose sight of love while leading your home, all parenting devolves into chores that are robbing you of something. It's this lack of love that twists an unbelievable gift, a child, into a taxing inconvenience.

Our generation has been told that kids ruin things—careers, travel, finances, and fun. I have heard many parents say that the difference between a vacation and a trip is whether kids are present. Even Christians propagate the narrative that kids take away more than they offer.

Yet I believe that kids don't ruin our lives as much as they reveal how selfish our desires tend to be. You are not the victim of your parenting responsibilities. You are the beneficiary.

Having kids recenters our lives on others instead of ourselves. And the only way to endure that transition without stress is to transform your egotistical conceit into a God-given, others-centered delight. Such love washes away stress. Love for your kids and your role in their lives makes what would otherwise be bothersome into a blessing. It's love that turns a labor into a gift. It didn't suddenly become any more convenient or any easier. Love just made it feel light.

I don't want you to *have* to lead your family. No, you are so free in Christ that you *get* to lead them—lovingly, inconveniently, and gladly. No one expects you to be perfect, but I do want you to be strong enough not to crumble under the pressure when you fail. The weight of parenting perfectly or even just well is more than any one of us can bear. "I can't do this!" is the cry of every parent at some point.

But Jesus says to the overburdened parent, "No, you can't. Not on your own. And you don't have to. You get to do this with me." In Christ, you are never parenting by yourself. Never. He never leaves. He never forsakes. He always helps. He strengthens. And as you'll see, he invites you to be unburdened, to find relief from all the pressures and stresses of parenting in his generous love.

The Drudgery Mindset

You are a parent, so I know you have hard days. You do what you're supposed to do even when you don't want to do it. It can be overwhelming at times. It takes a lot out of you. A lot of days it's both difficult and unsatisfying.

In a conversation I had not too long ago with a friend, I was complaining about the hardships of the particular stage of parenting I was in. Without thinking about what I was doing, I griped about how tough my life was because of my kids and their numerous needs and the constant demands and all the chores of caring for them. I described my family as if I was an unappreciated, overworked subordinate to my children.

The friend I was venting to was kind enough to look me in the eyes and compassionately confront my perspective. He was a childless man who had always wanted to be a dad. It was hard for him to listen to me complain about the complications of a privilege that he had always desired for himself. Seeing his longing to have the same challenges I was bemoaning touched my heart. It was like my eyes were opened, and I saw my grumbling for the ungrateful, unloving, and misguided protest that it was. God says that "children are a heritage from the Lord, the fruit of the womb a reward. Like arrows in the hand of a warrior are the children of one's youth. Blessed is the man who fills his quiver with them!" (Ps. 127:3–4). Yet I had turned the kids that God calls a personal reward into obstacles in my life story. I'd lost sight of love, and I was confusing blessings and burdens.

I'd tell anyone that fatherhood is wonderful. I love being my kids' dad. I wish everyone could have kids as enjoyable as mine and love them as thoroughly as I do. It would be no exaggeration on my part to say that I'd rather be a father than just about anything else in the world. And yet when I'm talking to my kids about their responsibilities or considering my own domestic duties, many days I treat such tasks as requirements instead of things to rejoice in. As magnificent as this lifelong parenting assignment is, for some reason it is second nature for me to turn the everyday moments of parenting into drudgery.

Drudgery is the kind of tedious, obnoxious, and often trivial work that no one wants to do. You keep doing it, but you wish you were doing something else. In a drudgery mindset, you parent because you need to parent, not because you love to parent. That's because our motivation is off. We're being driven not by love but by a sense of pressure. The pressure to get it all done. The pressure to succeed. The pressure to balance everything. The pressure to be as perfect as possible. And that pressure is what is stressing us out, not our kids themselves.

When we succumb to this pressure, we miss out on the sweet relief that comes from a home infused by the Spirit's love—the pleasant confidence, even in our imperfection, that we are not defeated just because our tasks are difficult or there are too many of them to balance. It's love from God for us and through us for others that creates a buoyancy in our burdens.

Beyond robbing my family of the gift of appreciating life together, having a drudgery mindset fosters an itch to complain and a tendency toward resentment. There's a constant temptation to grumble. It turns the honor of raising a child into an interruption of my preferred plan for my day and therefore something to resent and whine over. I keep parenting but am driven to it begrudgingly, as if I've been forced to against my will.

Leading a house under performance pressure robs your kids and you of the pleasure that should result from being part of a household that is free in Christ. We need relief from this pressure and drudgery mindset.

The love that Christians receive as a fruit of the Spirit is a gift for many reasons, but one of the sweetest blessings for parents is that love turns the difficult daily work of raising kids into something we do gladly and gratefully. It makes serving our children a delight, both for us and for our kids. Love makes the otherwise overwhelming requirements rewarding. Love relieves the pressure. Love transforms the drudgery. In short, caring *about* your family makes caring *for* them an honor and a pleasure.

Exercising Love

You would think freedom from drudgery would come from having less to do or getting more done in less time, a reduction in work or an increase in productivity. There can even be a false relief that comes from doing less. It feels like a relief to ignore our responsibilities, to procrastinate or forsake them altogether. It can't stress us out if we refuse to do them! But neglecting our parental duty will never bring true relief since the work needs to be done and we are the ones to do it. Relief isn't the same thing as being excused from doing hard things. Love doesn't always lead us to less labor. Sometimes love is the very reason to take on challenges and overcome them. Certainly, rhythms of rest and refreshment are an important part of taking care of yourself and your family. Yet there is also an abundance of relief in appreciating that the parenting work you need to do is not an obstacle to you but a way to exercise your love.

Thus, sometimes the relief is not in changing what you are doing but in embracing why you are doing it. Jesus didn't bend down to scrub Peter's feet out of a sense of begrudging obligation. Jesus served those who would soon reject him because he loved them. Love kept it from being drudgery. Love made it an example worth following. Love made it a joy to stoop to handle the dirty feet of those he led. Likewise, you can enjoy being a parent even in the most mundane and tedious tasks. Every aspect of the endless humdrum of the daily grind can be a blessing if seen through the filter of love.

Even menial, initially undesirable tasks we are doing for our kids can be consecrated as an offering of worship and thanksgiving to the

Lord. We can whip up a family meal and then wipe the saucy remnants of it off faces and fingers, tables and floors, walls and sometimes the ceiling—all as an offering to the Lord. We can do the dishes and then play the games and then read the stories for God. We can help with the homework and then listen to the complaint, change a diaper in the dark of night and fight fatigue in the light of day, take away a toy and give a hug—all to honor Jesus. We can do all this, confident that he sees each little task, he sees us, and he is pleased with our living sacrifice. So in that way, love for our God relieves the stress of doing all the things for our kids because regardless of what the temporal task is, it's all worship to the eternal Lord. It is all significant. It all matters. The love of God and love of neighbor blesses the name of the Lord. And blessing God is a blessing to us.

Did God give us kids to raise? Yes. Did he call us to raise our kids in a godly manner? Yes. But we shouldn't obey God out of fear of what would happen if we didn't. Nor should we obey begrudgingly, resenting the effort it takes. That's not freedom! Rather, a love of God should drive our obedience. In response to God's love, we should express genuine, full, immediate, loving obedience. A victorious, home-free family loves to obey God.

We all need to be reminded of this truth—that we can serve out of love thanks to God's love for us—because we get discouraged and are tempted to sin. No one has had to warn me to not eat dog food. I don't crave it. No one must tell me to not put my hand in the fire. I hate the pain of burning. But I do love sin. I do hesitate to serve others. I need to be warned. I need to be encouraged. I need my desires reset in order to align them with what God loves. Because I love God, I love to be faithful to him. I love to be a man of integrity. I don't obey God because I have to. I'm home-free. I follow God because I get to!

You also get to be obedient to God! Your God-given responsibilities are not a punishment for you. They are your liberation. There is nothing freer than obedience to a good King. His laws are a gift to you.

The Privilege of Being Parented

One of my sons once asked me if I was "born a grown-up." When we are little, we can't imagine our parents being anything other than adults. For Christians, however, our primary identity is not mom or dad but daughter or son—children of God! And God does not have a drudgery mindset about being our heavenly Father. He does not bemoan his constant care for us. He does not resent our neediness.

Consider this: There are times when I look at my children and have the most overwhelming sense of fondness for them. Have you ever experienced that? I look at them, and my heart swells with affection— my head swims with it. If this is true for me, and I'm an imperfect father, how much more so must God's affection and fondness run over for us? Do you realize this? First John 3:1 says, "See what kind of love the Father has given to us, that we should be called children of God; and so we are." Read that verse again. So we are *his children*, his beloved.

It's not that you first loved God but that he already loved you. He loves you with the kind of love that only a perfect, all-knowing Father could possess. There is not a single thing in all of existence—not your parenting, not your failures, not your past choices—that can separate you from the love of God.

And because he cares for you, he permits you to cast all your burdens on him. Remember what we talked about in chapter 1: According to Psalm 55:22, you can take the burdens and pressures that are weighing on you, and you can chuck (or *shalak*) them off. Hurl them down at the feet of God. God invites his people to be unburdened.

The New Testament quotes Psalm 55:22 to tell us why we can do this—because God "cares for you" (1 Pet. 5:7). Because *he* cares for *you*. This is ultimately why love is a relief from the stresses and pressures of parenting—it's not just your love from God for your family but God's love for you. Because you can cast every burden on the Lord, and because he can handle any burden, you can be relieved of what would otherwise overwhelm you. What is too much for you to carry alone can be hefted onto the God who loves you.

In turn, God grants us the capacity to love him back. Loving God is the greatest commandment and sets us free from all the pressures to please other masters.

If you are struggling with stress from life's pressures, as many of us are, the relief you need isn't found in procrastination. It's not found in productivity. It's not found in meeting the expectations of others. Those are false relief. The relief you need is found in faith. Faith in Jesus Christ. Faith that, because of his love, you are home-free. So trust that your Savior Jesus loves you—that he is eager to relieve your burdens. Your workload might grow, but so can your faith.

Sitting Down with Christ and the Angel

When there is pressure on us, we often respond to it with frenetic activity, spiraling thoughts, or numbing escapist entertainment and substances in an attempt to ignore our situation. When you're stressed, what do you do? What have you done to address your stress?

Have you ever tried sitting down and doing nothing? Not with a TV show on. Not with a book or device in your hands. Sitting down, committed to do nothing but breathe. Nothing but listen. As a society, we are terrible at this—especially when we are stressed. It's odd wisdom. *Try sitting!*

I'm not against hard work, and I'm not against planning ahead or enjoying something fun. Neither is Jesus, but I want you to consider Christ's current position, his posture even. Hebrews 10 describes the frenetic activity of the Jewish priests who daily repeated their rituals and sacrifices. They got up and worked all day, day after day. But Hebrews says such activity wasn't actually solving the problem they were trying to address—sin. Hence the need to get up the next day and do it all over again. Unlike them, Jesus Christ is seated. His work accomplished once for all what needed to be done. He is not frantically trying to solve the problems of your life. Even during his earthly ministry, Christ was not riding a horse from town to town, pleading with everyone to see and hear him. Rather, he sauntered across the Holy Land preaching his simple message of repentance and the kingdom of heaven, unhurried and unstressed. And now? He's seated. He is not fretting about how we'll solve yesterday's unfinished tasks, address today's curveballs, or prepare for tomorrow's potentialities. He's seated. With all the problems of the world, Jesus's life is still not hectic. You never see a frantic Jesus. You also never hear a whining Jesus.

Yes, in life he was strained. Because of his love for you, he was tested physically, mentally, emotionally, and spiritually. He endured the worst pains of this world, the worst kind of stress. He bled, he wept, he grieved, and he faced pervasive conflict. He resisted Satan's temptations and suffered under mankind's hostility. He was exhausted, hungry, rejected, and opposed. He was mocked, beaten, and abandoned. But he was never defeated by the strain.

And now what is his current posture? Is it a begrudging hassle for him to sort out your life? Is he scrambling to keep it all on track? According to Hebrews 1 and 10, Jesus is seated.

When Jesus was raised from the dead, Matthew tells us that an angel dressed in clothes like lighting came with an earthquake, rolled away what was probably a ferociously heavy rock from in front of the tomb, and then did what? He didn't blow a trumpet. There was no war cry. He didn't decapitate the Roman guards. He didn't go berserk on the doubters. He was not in an angelic frenzy. In fact, he was the opposite of agitated. Matthew says that the angel simply sat down on the stone. The Messiah had done exactly what he said he would do. The work was done, and the angel sat down.

How do you picture an angel sitting on a big stone? Are his legs dangling? Is he reclined? Does he have his feet kicked up? This is a little of what it looks like for a parent who has believed the good news.

The love of God relieves stress. We are at ease because of the finished work of Christ.

When was the last time you sat down just to remind yourself that God was in control? Try it. Sit down with Jesus. Take some time to do less and breathe deep. Exercise faith that Jesus's work on your behalf is completed. You have a seated Savior and an invitation to sit too. Remind yourself that God is in control. Listen to the invitation to be still for a time. Trust the Lord who loves you to be all-knowing since you can't be. Trust the Lord who loves you to be all-powerful since you can't be. Trust the Lord who loves you to be everywhere at once since you can't be. Feel his love wash over you. Be at ease even amid the work left to do. The angel sat on the stone. Christ sits on his throne. You are not alone.

A Prayer for Times of Overwhelming Stress

Heavenly Father, I confess that I am stressed. My patience is worn thin, my love has grown cold, and I get flustered. I am weary. I am run ragged.

Remind me to rest. When I slow down, recharge me. Give me a reinvigorated soul, and inspire me for the long days and nights with my family. Revitalize my mind and heart. Where my heart is hectic, bring genuine relief. Where the demands of my life have multiplied, protect me from getting burned out.

Transform the tasks of parenting from drudgery to delight through your rejuvenating love. Reframe my life for me, and help me see the blessing of this difficult calling. Release me from a victim mentality, and breed enjoyment in my heart. I want to serve my family and be fulfilled by my duties instead of frustrated. Forgive me for looking to myself to overcome what you've invited me to entrust to you. Amen.

Reflection Questions

1. What stresses you out about parenting?

2. If you are being honest, why do you do what you do for your kids?

3. What aspects of leading your household feel like chores and drudgery?

4. When you are tempted to grumble and gripe about your life, where do you take your complaints? How do you express them?

5. How do you think God feels about how he serves you? Is he stressed?

6. Where and when can you sit with Jesus to be restored?

Why should the children of a King
Go mourning all their days?
Great Comforter, descend, and bring
Some tokens of thy grace.

Dost thou not dwell in all the saints,
And seal the heirs of heaven?
When wilt thou banish my complaints,
And show my sins forgiven?

Assure my conscience of her part
In the Redeemer's blood;
And bear thy witness with my heart,
That I am born of God.

Thou art the earnest of his love,
The pledge of joys to come;
And thy soft wings, celestial Dove,
Will safe convey me home.

ISAAC WATTS
"The Witnessing and Sealing Spirit" (1709)

4

Joy

Relief from Despair

WHEN WE HOLD OUR BABIES in our arms for the first time, we call them "little bundles of joy." We waited a long time to meet them. They coo, and they snuggle. They look us in the eye, and our hearts swell.

Then they start to scream at us. They scream when they're hungry. They scream when they're tired. They scream when they're uncomfortable. Sometimes they scream for no perceivable reason. Then as they get older, they learn words to scream. They rebel. They demand. They reject. They refuse. In our frustration, do we still see them as bundles of joy?

Sometimes they get dirty. Sometimes they make a mess. Sometimes they get injured. Sometimes they get sick. Sometimes they get *scary* sick. Some of them sadly pass away before they even grow up. Some of them pass away before we ever even get to hold them. In our sorrow, do we still see them as bundles of joy?

When they turn the corner into young adulthood, we call them "our pride and joy." They're maturing and changing and deciding. They can talk with us about the things they like, and they can talk about all the things they don't like. Then one day *we* are what they don't like.

Their defiance matures too. Sometimes they make terrible decisions. Sometimes they want to get away. They want "freedom." To them, freedom is getting away from our rules, our opinions, our God, and us. In our brokenness, do we still see them as our pride and joy?

Parents are no strangers to the ache of despair, but with hope in Christ, even the deepest despair can find relief. Joy is the outcome of walking with God, and this joy is not fickle. There is no situation in which the believer cannot find joy. Did anyone face a greater challenge than Christ? And yet even in his strain and grief, he never lacked joy in the Father.

Conditional Feelings

Though we typically use "joy" and "happiness" interchangeably, they are not the same thing. Happiness is a gladness tied to what is happening. Unlike happiness, joy is a gladness that is not deterred by our circumstances. Joy is like an enormous oak tree. Its roots are spread out as far as its branches, gripping the earth, and it's almost impossible to move it from its territory. It's the definition of durable. Happiness, on the other hand, is like the shadow the tree casts on the ground around itself. It is constantly changing. As the sun moves across the sky, the shadow shifts shape and position and size. At night, the shadow may not be perceivable at all. Yet through every season, day and night, the tree still stands. Happiness is unstable. Joy is reliable.

I think I have a very happy life. When my kids are happy, I am happy, and they are happy a lot. When my marriage is fun, I am happy, and we have a lot of fun. When it's evident that my friends care about me, I am happy, and I have sweet friends. I am happy when I am right about something, and though that happens less often than I'd like, when it does happen, I am delighted.

If, however, things are not going how I want, I am not happy. Honestly, things don't go how I want a lot. So I am often unhappy. My happiness is not resilient. Happiness can abandon me in an instant.

Like you, I'm sure, I've had crushing, sad days. I've felt unloved. Unappreciated. Inadequate. Insulted. Ineffectual. Wrong. I've been lonely, jealous, and weak. And sometimes I've been sad for no particular reason I could put my finger on. I've had sad parenting days when my actions grieved me, my child's responses grieved me, or I just felt useless and unwanted.

I've also seen some of the most awful, agonizing, tragic depths of family sorrow. I've visited the deathbed of newborns. I've pleaded with teenagers who don't want to live anymore. I've housed adolescents who've been kicked out of their homes. I've prayed with the parents of terminally ill sons and daughters. I've processed stories of horrific abuse with the victims. I've helped children navigate their family's new dynamic after divorce. I've visited middle schoolers in jail. I've seen sons punch fathers in a rage. I've heard daughters curse their parents. I've heard mothers weep over their prodigal and defiant teenagers. I've mediated between spouses who despised each other.

Where the tombstones mark off days instead of years, where the graves are marked with toys and teddy bears, sadness is the right response. There is nothing happy about these situations. Nothing. I have often felt the pastoral pressure to have the right things to say in moments of deep hurt. But what words could possibly bring light into such a darkness?

Even though such tragic situations may be rare, misery is not uncommon for parents. With so much love and hope wrapped up in the life of a child, it's also the perfect recipe for profound disappointment, suffering, and hurt. The kinds of situations that make a parent's heart ache are apt to induce despair. Despair is a kind of deep sadness laced with a sense of hopelessness. Despair is a total lack of joy.

But there is a sweet relief from despair found in the Spirit of God. There must be. Otherwise, why would God tell us to "rejoice always" in 1 Thessalonians 5:16? Why would he say to "count it all joy, my brothers, when you meet trials of various kinds" in James 1:2 unless there could be joy in a variety of trials? Why would Paul reiterate this in Philippians 4:4 when he said, "Rejoice in the Lord always; again I will say, rejoice," if always rejoicing wasn't possible?

I want you to take a moment to read through 2 Corinthians 4:8 a few times right now: "We are afflicted in every way, but not crushed; perplexed, but not driven to despair." *Afflicted in every way. But not driven to despair.*

Conditional Faith

Despair, a sense of hopeless sorrow, is always a result of unbelief. You can think you are hopeless only if you think God is powerless or careless. When we don't believe that God is good and that God is in control, then we have no hope, and that is when we are tempted to despair, to not trust that God's victory applies anymore. When our suffering has overwhelmed us, it is because despair has outgrown our faith. And that is when we parent as though we are not free, not protected, and might lose—as though we are anything but home-free.

There is such great news for parents who are struggling with despair: Hope and joy are available to us in Christ. Jesus describes it in John 16:22 as a joy that no one can take away from you. This joy can always be found by trusting Christ in all things.

Unlike despair, joy comes from belief. Plain and simple. Joy is something constant and settled in us. It is not a reaction, and it doesn't fluctuate. Happiness and sadness come and go. In Christ, joy is not conditional. It's not conditional because it is tied to our faith in Christ and because God is unchanging. In faith, our sadness and sorrow never eclipse our hope. When tragedy has pierced us so deeply that our soul cries out, "But why?" we can rejoice that God has not lost control. He comforts us in our pain and has compassion for us in our struggles. Even in our darkest moments, the darkness has not overcome our faith. We are still home-free. We are still more than conquerors.

Joy is our relief from despair, but where can we find it? Joy will be unobtainable if we look for it to be manufactured by our own hearts.

Joy is not born in us; it is given to us. Joy will be impossible to keep if we equate it to our happiness, which, unlike joy, is inexorably tied to our changing circumstances. On the other hand, joy will be impervious to depreciation if it is affixed to us by Christ. God does not come and go from his people, and so neither does his joy. God's power does not wax and wane in our lives, and so neither does his joy. God's plan for us does not have to adjust or adapt to new events, and so neither does his joy. Joy is the result of walking by the Spirit. Our joy is melded to our faith in God, and therefore it can endure, immune to any environmental changes.

What a gift! Walking with God gives us an imperishable gladness. Many of our feelings are conditional. They change based on our situation. But if you have a feeling that is tethered to something immutable, you can expect that feeling to persist regardless of circumstances. This is the case with Christian joy. The gladness in our hearts is tied to our faith in God's goodness and sovereignty, two of the attributes of his very being.

A Transactional Relationship with the Almighty

Yet the relationship that God invites us into is not based on bartering or quid pro quo. That's a transactional relationship, which is based on exchanges and attempts to satisfy individual desires that are mutually beneficial. Despair is often the result of trying to have a transactional relationship with God, in which we offer him something out of our desire to sway our circumstances in our favor.

Faith and obedience are not currencies, but for some reason, we are apt to treat them as such. I will give you praise if you give me what I want. I will pray if you give me the answer I want. I will trust you as long as things go as I wish. I will give you credit if you keep me happy. I will confess my sin if you protect my reputation. I will walk in integrity if it benefits me. If I am discouraged or disappointed or suffering or uncomfortable, I will critique you. I will ignore you. I will abandon you for something I can control more easily. I will give only if I can receive. My feelings and my behavior are tied to whether I'm getting any benefits. I have to get and keep if I'm going to faithfully follow. We treat God like a wishing well, putting in our currency (hopefully not too much) and praying that we get what we want.

We'll know our relationship with God is transactional when what he can offer us is more important than who he is (we didn't get what we want, so we don't trust him) or when our will being done is a prerequisite for our obedience to his commands (we don't follow God because obedience doesn't get us the results we seek). When we treat our relationship with God transactionally and we don't get what we want, it leads us into a faith crisis.

In this kind of relationship, we will be tempted to despair because, in reality, we have nothing to offer God in order to get what we want. Such despair is based on a false assumption that he might be looking to charge us for his love and care.

Faith and obedience are not things we offer God as incentives to get him to fashion the life we want out of the one we have. Faith is believing that the potter knows better than the clay what should be done, even when there are unexpected or unwanted twists in the act of sculpting or in the use of the sculpture. Faith says, "I will do whatever you want no matter what. I trust you." When our commitment to God gets tangled up with whether we are safe, secure, and satisfied to our liking, we are not walking by the Spirit but demanding that the Spirit walk by us.

Unlike Job, our heart cries out, "The Lord gives, but he had better not take away!" (cf. Job 1:21). We hitch our faith to the provision of safety and success. We believe the Lord is good when he gives, but he can't still be good and take away. Our hearts are tied to receiving and keeping. Sin convinces us that there is no losing what is precious and still keeping our joy.

Of course, no one wants this kind of transactional relationship with their own children. What if they bartered their behavior for favors? "If you make the kind of dinner I like, Mom and Dad, then I won't lie, cheat, or steal this week. If you let me do whatever I want tonight, then I won't slander you to my friends or their parents. But if I can't get what I want, then you can expect my behavior to be the worst it's ever been!" Is obedience or honoring parents a negotiable in your household? I hope not. You know that good parenting requires your children to do things they don't want to do and to give up things they want to keep. You know that in the parent-child relationship, you carry a weight of responsibility to foster obedience for the good of your child.

If you, a flawed mom or dad, would not run your household like a negotiation, if you wouldn't make obedience a bargaining chip because you know that genuine obedience is done out of love and trust, how much more must your heavenly Father want a relationship with you that isn't built on haggling transactions? How much more should we trust a perfect Father who knows all and oversees all? And what joy is available to the family whose hope is secure in Christ no matter what?

What if what God has for you is years of agony and grief? What if what God has in store for you is suffering? Our God has told you that in him there is joy in every circumstance, even in trials. By trusting him, obeying him, and committing to him, you will have a gladness undeterred by sorrow. Criticizing God is not faith. Confidence in God is faith. And in our Christian confidence, we will find the unshakable joy that God gives to his people.

All we have that we can offer to God is ourselves. We give him our trust and surrender our lives, and in the assurance of his power and love, there is hope and joy.

But Why?

For almost all of us Christians, when we find ourselves in the midst of profound suffering or despair, we seek meaning and explanation. We look to God and say simply and desperately, "But why?"

In Luke 13 there is a group of people who ask Jesus a similar question about why some awful event had taken place. In verses 4–5, Jesus poses a question back to the crowd about another tragedy, in which some people were crushed and killed by a falling tower: "Do you think that they were worse offenders than all the others who lived in Jerusalem? No, I tell you; but unless you repent, you will all likewise perish." The explanation Christ gives amid tragedy is that we should not assume that every tragedy is a result of cosmic karma, by which bad people endure bad calamities. Instead, we should see in every tragedy a call to repent, knowing that every one of us may soon face our God to give an account.

In John 9, Jesus's disciples ask him about a man born blind. They ask if it is because of his sin or maybe even the sin of his parents that he has never been able to see. Jesus answers, "It was not that this man sinned, or his parents, but that the works of God might be displayed in him" (9:3). Jesus interprets this suffering and blindness as something that will bring glory to God. While that might be easy to see in the moment of the miracle, many might say, "But why was he blind since birth? Would God not have had as much glory if he had let the man see for most of his life?" We all find ways that we think God could do things differently in order to better meet our needs. Do we trust God with determining our lives? If we truly do, we will find that inside that trust is the relief that only joy can bring regardless of circumstances.

As Christians, we believe that we live in a world that is not as it should be. This world was created "very good" (Gen. 1:31). It was as it should have been. But it is not that way now. It has been corrupted by sin. We are corrupted by sin. We also believe that this world will one day be the way it should be again. It will be very good again. In the meantime, we will trust the God who made a way to overcome what is broken in our world and in ourselves.

Our joy is not rooted in some clear explanation of *why* we suffer but in whom we place our trust *when* we suffer. We don't need a reason from God for why a bad thing has happened but rather the assurance that God is faithful and can be trusted through it all. When we are tempted to look to God and ask, "But why?" let us remember that God is wise, good, and gracious and that he does not cause the world's brokenness but rather is the source of its renewal and redemption.

Is It Sinful to Be Sad?

Both in my children and in me, I've seen a temptation to hide sadness or to say, "I'm sorry that I'm sad." But sadness doesn't always require an apology. It can actually be the right response to sad circumstances. One of my favorite writers and pastors, Zack Eswine, teaches that sadness in a sad situation is a sign that your heart is working properly. He says, "In this fallen world, sadness is an act of sanity, our tears the testimony of the sane."[1] Thus, a sad heart doesn't need fixing; it needs comfort. There is no need to confront sadness in others. To comfort, yes. But to confront? Only with compassion and sensitivity.

A Christian parent will probably experience profound sorrow and sadness, but this is not always indicative of a crisis of faith. We know from God's word that it is okay to mourn, to grieve, and to lament. These emotions may not be permanent, but they are inevitable for every follower and family.

We are often tempted to fix, hide, or correct sadness. But sometimes it's okay just to sit in sadness. Of course, it's also okay to not be sad and to recover from sadness. There is a kind of sick and twisted attention seeking that can come in the form of sulking and whining that we should avoid as believers. Sadness like that should be cast off. We should not revel in sadness or exploit it, looking for someone to feed our hungry ego, but neither should the existence of selfish sadness tempt us to shun it altogether.

Even in sadness, however, we never lose the fruit of joy because God has not and will not take away his banner of victory over our lives. What God teaches us is that though happiness and sorrow are

---

1   Zack Eswine, *Spurgeon's Sorrows: Realistic Hope for Those Who Suffer from Depression* (Christian Focus, 2015), 19.

incompatible, joy and sorrow can coexist. Joy is a constant, and sorrow is an inevitability.

Sorrow is expressed by what we call lament. Unless it is Good Friday or Ash Wednesday, it is likely that when your church gathers, it does not sing songs of lament together. But there are many expressions of godly grief and sorrow in your Bible. The book of Psalms has several chapters of lament that express longing for God during times of distress, desperation, trouble, and waiting. Consider Psalm 102:4, where the psalmist says, "My heart is struck down like grass and has withered," or Psalm 13:2, where the psalmist asks, "How long must I take counsel in my soul and have sorrow in my heart all the day?" The Psalms teach that it is safe to cry out to God with your heart's aching. God is never surprised by your anguish or disturbed by your distress.

In fact, Christ himself grieved. His sadness coexisted with joyful faith. Like you, Jesus had sad days. In Isaiah 53:3, the prophet tells us that the Messiah was a "man of sorrows and acquainted with grief." Jesus wept over Jerusalem. He wept over the death of his friend Lazarus. He agonized in the garden of Gethsemane. But unlike you and me, Jesus had a perfect joy that was complete. His joy was rooted not in his circumstances but in his perfect, steadfast relationship with the Father, which he has now generously offered to share with us. So now, like Jesus, we can have a joyful attachment to the God of all comfort even in our sadness.

If, as you read this chapter, you find yourself in a very dark place, I hope you will receive this comforting truth—through union with Christ, God is with you. He is near to the brokenhearted. Not that he is ever far, but he does have a tender heart for his sons and daughters who suffer. He comes alongside his suffering followers, and he shepherds them into and out of whatever may come. Your tears are seen. Your cries are heard. Your soul is cared for. Even in your sadness, you have hope that laces your grief with joy.

Sometimes life is so hard that it feels as though God, if he is real, must be cruel or absent or impotent. In Isaiah 49:14, the people of

God cry out, "My Lord has forgotten me!" God responds by saying that a nursing mom is more likely to forget her baby than God is to forget his people. In other words, God emphatically declares, "I will *not* forget you!"

In this passage, God compares himself with a breastfeeding mother. A mother's heart is full of love for her nursing child. This mother is more likely to leave her hungry baby than God is to leave his people. The best mother's love is only an imperfect picture of God's love for you. You may be suffering, but you are not forgotten, you are not abandoned, and God has not lost control of your story.

When we cry out to God in distress, "Why aren't you doing something about this?" he says that everything that needs to be done has been done. That's why he sent his Son, Jesus. Let me remind you of his great love for you, and let that be the fountain of joy and hope in your despairing, sorrowful soul. It's not that God has forgotten you. If anything, it's that we have forgotten what God is like. If our God would give his Son's life for you, would he do that only to then forsake you? Romans 8:32 says, "He who did not spare his own Son but gave him up for us all, how will he not also with him graciously give us all things?"

Further, though there is joy for us in the present, there is also a sweet promise of a future joy when it no longer coexists with sorrow. The prophet Isaiah tells us in Isaiah 25:8 that God "will swallow up death forever; and the Lord GOD will wipe away tears from all faces, and the reproach of his people he will take away from all the earth, for the LORD has spoken." There is coming a day when there will be nothing left to grieve and no sin left to correct. As the voice from the throne says in Revelation 21:4, God "will wipe away every tear from [our] eyes, and death shall be no more, neither shall there be mourning, nor crying, nor pain anymore, for the former things have passed away." In this life we have joy mingled with our pain, but there is a day coming when only joy shall remain. Look at the intimate tenderness of your God.

He approaches you close enough to wipe away the tears from your face. Oh, what joy there is for the ones who trust in Jesus!

There is nothing more grievous than losing someone you love. This is why the greatest joy I can imagine is this resurrection joy! Imagine the leaping heart of Mary Magdalene when she saw her beloved teacher, Jesus, back from the dead after three days! The reality of Christ conquering death together with the promise of resurrection for all those who believe is our greatest joy.

I don't need to teach you a joy mantra or a joy ritual or a joy habit for your times of despair. It's not a better joy tactic that you need; it's Jesus! The Spirit of God in you cannot be shaken loose. If you know Jesus, turn to him. In him you will find a joy that no sorrow can erase.

There is a false hope that comes from looking for the silver lining in every circumstance. Our joy is not built on whether we can find some good among a whole lot of bad. Our joy is built on the person, work, and promises of Jesus Christ. Those promises are good for all times, no matter how hideous, and they give us hope and joy.

If you are struggling with despair, the relief you need isn't found in silver linings, it's not found in success, and it's not found in godless coping mechanisms. Those are false relief. The relief you need is found in faith. Faith in Jesus Christ. Faith that because of his love, you are home-free. Trust that your Savior Jesus has a joy that can be made complete for you and that he is eager to comfort you in your despair. Your suffering might increase, but so does faith.

Take a moment right now and confess the times you have lacked hope. The times you allowed sorrow to reign. The times when joy evaded you.

For just a moment, put your fingers on your neck and feel your pulse. You have a heart pumping life through you, even when you ignore it. The Spirit offers you joy to walk with him, even when it seems muted and far away—even when you fail to notice or when circumstances are so dark that it seems hopeless. He always walks with you.

A Prayer for Times of Despair

Heavenly Father, I am utterly defeated. There is no strength in me to press on. It feels as though the darkness has overcome the light, and I'm left without hope.

Redeem my pain. Show me how my plight matters. Help me see you and feel you. You say you are near to the brokenhearted. My heart is broken. Be nearby. You are the God of all comfort, so please comfort me.

Give me a resilient gladness and a faith that endures. Restore joy to me and invite me into your peace. I rely on your promises. My confidence is built on you. I believe you make all things new. I believe in the resurrection. Show me Jesus and his pierced hands lifting me back to my feet. Amen.

Reflection Questions

1. What parts of your story are the darkest?

2. How do you lament?

3. Where do you put your faith when life is hard?

4. Whom do you turn to when you are discouraged? What would they have to say to touch your heart?

5. How does God address your sadness and hurt?

6. If you had a friend who was struggling with despair, what do you think you could do that would bless that individual?

Calm me, my God, and keep me calm,
Let thine outstretched wing
Be like the shade of Elim's palm
Beside her desert spring.

Yes; keep me calm, though loud and rude
The sounds my ear that greet;
Calm in the closet's solitude,
Calm in the bustling street;

Calm in the hour of buoyant health,
Calm in my hour of pain;
Calm in my poverty or wealth,
Calm in my loss or gain;

Calm in the sufferance of wrong,
Like Him who bore my shame;
Calm 'mid the threatening, taunting throng,
Who hate Thy holy name;

Calm me, my God, and keep me calm,
Soft resting on Thy breast;
Soothe me with holy hymn and psalm,
And bid my spirit rest.

HORATIUS BONAR
"Calm Me, My God, and Keep Me Calm" (1857)

5

Peace

Relief from Anxiety

CHILDREN HAVE WILD IMAGINATIONS. Though they've never seen unicorns and dragons in real life, they can see them in their minds. Kids imagine monsters that seem very real (even when they're not). They love to pretend. They pretend to have magical powers that give them superhuman strength and speed. They pretend to be cooks and astronauts, race car drivers and doctors, explorers and entertainers. They even pretend to be parents sometimes.

Parents have wild imaginations too. Though we've never seen mythical creatures in real life, we imagine a world full of perfect moms and perfect dads. We imagine monsters—bullies, kidnappers, and diseases—that seem very real (even when they're not). Parents love to pretend too. We pretend we have our own magical powers, our own superhuman strengths. We pretend we can see the future. We pretend things would be better if we could control everything. We pretend that if we worry enough, then we can guarantee the safety of those we love.

Of course, there are very real struggles and dangers that we face as families. It's their very real potential that plagues us. In a sense, parents do deal with actual monsters. But one of the greatest challenges we meet as parents is overcoming our fixation with hypothetical threats. Parental preoccupation with *potential* problems is a *real* problem. It's a form of anxiety. Anxiety is an agonizing worry over whether we will get or keep what we want. Anxiety is a liar and an insidious tormentor.

Praise God that our worst anxious thoughts can be relieved by the peace that comes from walking by the Spirit. It's God's peace that can tame the wild imaginations of moms and dads and calm our otherwise restless hearts.

Pessimistic Parenting

Most parents have an overdeveloped talent for pessimistic risk assessment. This can make us *hyper*vigilant. Maybe like me, you are on high alert in public places with your kids. I attribute it to how many counseling sessions I've had with people who've been through horrific trials of abduction and abuse. If there is a strange adult or even an unknown child near my kids, my antennae are up, and my eyes are peeled.

My family was once almost the victim of an accidental kidnapping. My youngest son was playing on a crowded playground when an older man came up to him and gently said, "Come on. It's time to go," and reached out to take my son's hand. Mind you, this was done right in front of me. Before this, I had mentally readied myself for a million dangerous circumstances but never one that came so mildly. You'd think a prepared dad like me would slap the man's hand away or deliver a swift uppercut to the would-be abductor. That I'd twist his scrawny, wrinkled arm behind his back and call the police. That at the very least, I'd step between him and my son, eyes ablaze with righteous paternal fury.

Of all the things I could have said to ward off a potential kidnapper, the only thing that came out of my mouth was, and this was in the weakest tone you can imagine, "Nope. That's my son." Despite my mild-mannered protest, he ignored what I said, smiled at me, and reissued the grandfatherly invitation for my son to go with him. But I was gently and respectfully resolute. This kid was definitely my child, and he wasn't going anywhere with a stranger, no matter how kindly he was asked.

This grandpa was obviously confused, surely a case of mistaken identity. I can only hope that he eventually found the right grandson to take home. All I know is that he didn't get far with one of my boys. Crisis averted. I'm a real hero, if you think about it—the world's most considerate crime fighter.

Maybe abductions don't concern you. But when it comes to parenting, if it's not one thing, then it's another. When you care about something, you will always be worried about it, and if it's not one thing, then it's everything all at once. If it's not our children's physical well-being, it's their emotional health. *Are my children happy?* If it's not their health, it's their development. *Are they on track?* If it's not their development, then it's their socializing. *Do my kids have friends?* If it's not our kids, then it's ourselves. *Am I balancing work and home? Am I too harsh or too soft? Am I sleeping well? Eating well? Leading well?* Just about anything, real or imagined, can make us anxious. Parental pessimism is literally boundless.

You Should Be Terrified

In the process of becoming a church planter, I underwent some hefty formal evaluations. My wife and I attended a weekend event at which we were asked innumerable questions, had to solve difficult hypothetical situations, and shared our vision for a new church, which was all then analyzed by a review board. The first part of this long process was preaching to a few dozen pastors and then receiving their immediate critiques of my skills. I was as nervous as I could ever remember being. It felt to me as if so much was riding on this one sermon. Our potential church, my livelihood, my family's future, and even my value as a person were all at stake.

Just before I got up to speak, my wife asked me if I was nervous.

"Of course!" I said.

"Are you worried about what these people will think about you?"

"Absolutely," I responded.

What I expected to hear next was some encouragement or some major vote of confidence, a sentiment of vigorous support, a rousing spousal "You got this!" with an optional slap on the back or a kiss on the cheek (her choice). Instead, she said, "Then you should be nervous. You should be terrified." Admittedly, I was a little confused at first.

She locked eyes with me and continued, "If you think that preaching God's word or starting a church is about your ability to impress other people, then we *should* be scared. If this work is all about you, then we shouldn't do this at all. But if you are ready to serve God with your sermon, as you should, then get up there and share his word for his glory without being so concerned about yours." (My wife is the best.)

I was obsessing over the dangers and risks inherent in a job that depended on me. In that moment, I needed to have my gaze widened and my perspective challenged. My eyes needed to be pointed up. I still wanted to do well, but there was no benefit from all the worrying. Anxiety comes from confusion about who is in control and what our limits are.

I struggle with this confusion all the time when it comes to parenting. Parenting makes me anxious because, with all the responsibility, I feel as if my family's happiness, safety, success—all of it—depends on me. Or parenting makes me anxious because of the egotistical dread that comes from realizing I can't make it depend on me. The truth is, we all depend on God. And God does not depend on any of us.

Any time life depends on me getting anything exactly right, everyone should brace themselves for disappointment. If my family really does ultimately depend on me, then I do have a lot to fear. I should be terrified. I am weak and incapable of saving myself, let alone my children. It's okay to want to do a good job, to work hard at managing my responsibilities, to put in every ounce of effort I've got, but if my future or my family's future depends solely on me, I might as well be fighting a fire-breathing dragon with a stick of butter.

In parenting, anxiety often looks like obsessing over hypothetical events that could ruin everything. We seek a mythological "balance" in which we get everything right. We spend enormous amounts of mental energy trying to circumvent potential hazards or lamenting their existence. We overestimate the threats our family faces, and we underestimate the God who is for us, not against us. Doing that will always lead to anxiety.

A crisis of any size, real or imagined, can make us feel afraid. Fear is the natural response to something scary. If you are hoping to make it through life without any pain or suffering, then there will be a lot to be anxious about. If you are basing your approval and sense of peace on the opinions of others, then you'll have a lot to fear. You should be terrified. What one person loves about your parenting, another will criticize. You simply can't please everyone all the time. In fact, you can't please *anyone* all the time. You won't be undefeated.

In parenting we are facing a boulder too heavy for us to move, an enemy too strong for us to overcome, a task too difficult for us to complete, and a journey too long for us to finish. We should be terrified if everything depends on us. Praise God it doesn't!

A Pacified Heart

On the list of all-time greatest inventions, you have to include the printing press, light bulbs, and the internet. Personally, I also include things like air conditioning and indoor plumbing. I admit that it may not be in most people's top ten inventions in the history of the world, but somewhere on that list, as far as I'm concerned, should be the pacifier. I don't know if I would have survived the first few years of parenthood without one. The pacifier is aptly named. To a screaming, panicked child, it is a comfort that quiets his voice and his mind. It reassures him. It soothes. Everything is okay.

There is a word for this in Greek—*peithō*. It is very similar in meaning to our English word "reassure." It means "to be persuaded or convinced" and leads to peace. The word is used throughout the New Testament, though it is translated as several different words in English. Sometimes it is translated as "confidence," other times as "trust" or "assure," but most of the time as "sure" or "persuaded."

It's the word that Paul uses in Romans 8:38–39 when he says that he is "sure" that "neither death nor life, nor angels nor rulers, nor things present nor things to come, nor powers, nor height nor depth, nor anything else in all creation, will be able to separate us from the love of God in Christ Jesus our Lord." Paul is persuaded, convinced, confident, and therefore at peace because he knows that nothing in existence is more powerful than God and that, in Christ, God loves us. Paul's heart is sure and therefore pacified.

Romans 8:38–39 is the pacifier for the Christian's anxious heart. It soothes. We are sure. Confident. Convinced. Pacified. Everything is okay. Nothing in this world is more powerful than our God, and our God loves us. He is undefeated. He is confident and close at hand. We can depend on his love for us and his plan for our family. We can be confident in God's love in Christ Jesus.

Remember God's power over your story. In Christ, you are living in a story of mercy and peace, not panic. Even when we are not okay, everything is okay. Even when everything hurts on the inside, everything is okay. Even when our body fails us, everything is okay. Even when our worst fears are realized, everything is okay. Be convinced. Be at peace. The love of God soothes the heart of the anxious parent. And anxious parents can depend on God and let go of the lie that everything depends on them.

The Presence of Peace

Most of us parents think of "peace" as the absence of something. Maybe it's the absence of suffering, conflict, worry, or toil. To us, peace is the welcome void that's left when negative things go away. We often use the word "peace" paired with "quiet" as a description of what we want in our homes, usually implying the absence of our children's needs and noises.

But what if peace is more than just when your kids aren't bothering you? What if the fruit that God gives you is more than noise cancellation? What if peace isn't just for when things are going the way you want? What if the peace God gives you by walking with him isn't the absence of something at all? What if the fruit of walking with God is the presence of something—something very rare and extraordinarily precious to a parent?

Peace is not just the absence of disruption or suffering. It is the steadfast presence of wholeness and contentment—and not just a contentment that comes from having enough stuff but contentment from knowing Jesus is with you and is enough. Peace is knowing that Jesus sees and cares and is not afraid. That Jesus can be trusted. That in Christ, you are whole. Nothing is missing. Nothing is lacking. Nothing can be taken away. The presence of peace means finding contentment everywhere you formerly would have found concern.

What would it feel like if you were content even though your family wasn't perfect? Can you imagine what it would feel like if you were content even if your child wasn't experiencing a utopian upbringing? God creates peace not by eliminating the threat of suffering or taking away trouble but by increasing contentment, which flows from faith in him.

The root of all anxiety, and the root of all conflict, is discontentment. Discontentment is a lack of satisfaction with the way things are or a preemptive dissatisfaction with the way things might be. It is an insecurity that says, "I don't have what I need. I don't have enough. My assets are insufficient." Peace is the opposite of such insecurity. It is a confidence that the resources afforded to me are enough. When we underestimate God and what we can do in him, then we are afraid and anxious. When we have a right estimation of our ability to cope with our circumstances in Christ, we will find peace. Even in meager supply of what we want, even in injury and pain, even with diminished expectations for our future, we have a contentment and therefore peace that no circumstance can touch.

Who Cares?

On the wall of my office, I have a print of Gustave Doré's engraving *Jesus Calms the Storm*. It's an amazing work of art that I often consider when I'm feeling anxious and overwhelmed. It depicts the events of Mark 4:35–41, when the disciples are caught in a storm and terrified that they are about to die. In Doré's piece, the disciples are expressive and dramatic. They are desperate, panic stricken, and distraught with alarm. Jesus, on the other hand, sits calmly at the stern of the boat, totally confident and composed in the middle of the storm. Our seated Savior. I so badly want to be as assured as Jesus. Doré even portrays one disciple as being held back from Christ. We assume he is the one to voice the accusation of Jesus recorded in verse 38: "Do you not care?"

Next to that print in my office hangs another of Gustave Doré's engravings, an etching of Luke 10:38–42 titled *Jesus at the House of Martha and Mary*. In this story, a stressed, burdened Martha utters the same question as the overwhelmed disciples did at sea: "Do you not care?" (10:40). She challenges our seated Savior with her anxiety. She is frantic, while her sister is just sitting there.

The disciples on the boat and Martha in her house both confronted Jesus with the same question. It's one we often pray, either implicitly or explicitly. In frustration, in fear, or in desperation, we ask God, "Are you not concerned about what I'm concerned about?"

On the sea, Jesus said to the storm, "Peace! Be still!" (Mark 4:39). The wind and the waves obeyed him, and probably the hearts of his companions did too. Honestly, my heart often needs its storm commanded. I need to hear Jesus say to me, "Peace! Settle down. Sit still." This mind of mine, so muddled with the potential scenarios over which I have no control, needs to be stilled. The peace that Jesus has isn't because he doesn't care. He is at peace because he knows he is cared for by the Father. There's a false relief that says peace will be ours only if we stop caring so much. Care as much as you want! But don't worry, for as much as you care about your family, your heavenly Father cares even more about you, your spouse, and your children, and he is writing your story.

In Martha's house, Jesus says to her, "Martha, Martha, you are anxious and troubled about many things, but one thing is necessary" (Luke 10:41). The reason Martha's story in particular touches my heart is that it is easy to imagine myself in her shoes needing to hear what she heard. We utter a frantic cry to Jesus, "Aren't you concerned about what I'm concerned about? Look how hard this is right now!" And what better response could we hope for than to be seen in the way Jesus sees Martha, to hear what Martha heard?

When the burdens, real or imagined, of being a dad have overwhelmed me again, what greater privilege could I hope for than to hear him say my name and then repeat it: "Adam, Adam." Imagine it for yourself. Amid your concern, the uneasiness that your fear has fostered, Jesus looks at you and says your name. "You are troubled and anxious about so many things," he says.

You want to be understood at the ground level of your anxious soul. To be seen. To have your disquiet recognized and acknowledged. To be invited by your seated Savior to sit for a time. Hear Jesus's response. He cares, but he is not concerned. In other words, he is fully aware of what concerns us, but unlike us, he does not fret. Jesus never frets. Jesus is never anxious. Unlike us, he is the one on which everything—everything!—really does depend, and unlike us, he is not worried.

He does not wring his hands hoping for a future that's not yet settled. What is happening is not too hard for him. He has nothing to fear.

Now if he has nothing to fear and if he is with us and will never forsake us, what have we to fear?

Jesus does not just call us out of anxiety; he calls us to something better. What is the one thing Jesus recommends in the midst of troubling anxiety? Sitting and listening to his word. That is what Mary was doing. I am not against working or serving, but it must be done in light of Jesus's teachings. The word of God is the good news that the human heart needs. Try sitting. Try listening.

Try it right now. Sit down. Settle down. Place your hands in front of you, open and palms up. Hand your concerns to Christ, and listen to him call your name. Breathe deep. "_____, _____, you are troubled and anxious about so many things."

Now, hear what Jesus says in John 14:27: "Peace I leave with you; my peace I give to you. Not as the world gives do I give to you. Let not your hearts be troubled, neither let them be afraid." Read that again. Sit and listen to his words.

A Prayer for Relief from Anxiety

Heavenly Father, I am troubled and anxious about so many things. My mind is muddled by all that might happen. I am up to my neck in concerns. Pacify my restless heart. Steady my thoughts as you steady my breathing.

Remind me that you care. Remind me that you see me. Remind me that you have me and that no one has wrestled me away from you. Remind me of your presence and how you called me to abide here with you.

I want to sit as calmly as Christ did in the boat. I want to be impervious to this storm. Set me free from the persistent worry of my troubled mind. Clear my vision, and let me see you there guiding me. Help me trust you to lead me through this. Amen.

Reflection Questions

1. What ongoing troublesome situations do you worry about?

2. Where do you see pessimism in your parenting?

3. What comes to mind for you when you hear the word "peace"?

4. Are there any areas of your life where you are not trusting God and it is causing anxiety?

5. What would change in your mind and heart if you gave your worries to Christ?

6. How can you find contentment everywhere you find concern right now?

With tearful eyes I look around:
Life seems a dark and stormy sea;
Yet 'midst the gloom I hear a sound,
A heavenly whisper, "Come to Me!"

It tells me of a place of rest;
It tells me where my soul may flee;
Oh! To the weary, faint, opprest,
How sweet the bidding, "Come to Me!"

"Come; for all else must fail and die:
Earth is no resting-place for thee.
To heaven direct thy weeping eye:
I am thy portion; come to Me!"

O voice of mercy, voice of love!
In conflict, grief, and agony,
Support me, cheer me from above,
And gently whisper, "Come to Me!"

CHARLOTTE ELLIOTT
"Come to Me" (1882)

6

Patience

Relief from Exhaustion

SOMETIME SOON, SOMEONE WILL ASK YOU, "How are you?" For generations now the acceptable answers from parents are a thought-less "I'm good" or "Busy." That might be followed by one or more short complaints about an overfull life: "I'm worn out." "I'm tired." "I'm exhausted." "I'm beat." "I'm sapped." "I'm spent." "I'm bushed." "I'm drained." "I'm out of gas." "I'm swamped." "There aren't enough hours in the day." "I'm always rushing from one thing to the next." "I'm burning the candle at both ends." "I've got too many irons in the fire." "I've got a full plate."

Unlike despair, anxiety, shame, and fear, it doesn't take much to get a mom or dad talking about busyness or exhaustion. We will discuss our weariness and our overburdened schedules with just about anyone at any time. Real or imagined, "overworked" is how we see ourselves (or at least how we don't mind being seen). It's a struggle that is so broadly shared by and accepted among parents that you could argue we even admire it. We practically boast about our lack of sleep and the fullness of our calendars. We work to foster the mystique of "getting it all done."

Imagine if you asked another parent, "How are you?" and in response he said something like "I'm good. I'm not busy. I've got a lot of spare time. I've got more energy than I need, and I'm looking for more to do. I'm feeling strong. I'm in no hurry. I've got a lot left in the tank." Can you even imagine that? What would happen if someone asked you how you're doing, and you said anything like that? She might think you had gone crazy. Maybe she'd think you are the most refreshingly honest person she's talked to, someone who refuses to play the hurried parent game, someone who doesn't think busier is always better—either that or *You've lost your mind.*

Parental workloads are big, the lack of rest is real, and the pressure to do it all is crushing. We feel overloaded. But praise God—the strain of exhaustion can be relieved by the power of patience.

Patience as Grit

The truth is that most of us parents are genuinely tired people. And the more tired we are, the more we are easily annoyed. Exhaustion leads to fragility and a brittle mood. When our patience reserves are drained, we respond poorly. The more worn out we are, the shorter our temper and the more patience we then demand from our families.

I no longer use the same definition of "patience" that I used to teach to my kids when they were younger. For the Griffins, patience meant "waiting quietly and kindly." I often asked for this kind of patience from my kids. If I was in a conversation with another adult, patience meant they should not interrupt. If we were driving somewhere, patience meant not asking how much longer until we arrived. If there was a gift under the Christmas tree, patience meant not pestering me with guesses about what was inside.

An astute outside observer might notice that my demands for patience in my kids were often less than holy. To me, "patience" meant not bothering me while I was doing something important but waiting until I was done. It was basically a call not to be a nuisance. Ironically, asking my kids for patience was demonstrating my own lack of it. I was asking them to forsake what they wanted because I didn't want to forsake what I wanted. My requests for patience were a result of my impatience.

Sometimes my brittle mood couldn't handle being interrupted, being asked a repeated question, or being distracted from what I wanted to do. In telling my kids to be patient, I was demanding that they accept my inability or refusal to address their needs. The Bible has a word for that: "hypocrisy." I was asking them to do something that I wasn't willing to do—in this case, endure.

I mentioned that "waiting quietly and kindly" is not the definition of patience that I use anymore. It's not that I disagree with that definition—it's partly accurate. But it doesn't capture the full meaning of the word. It's missing a critical aspect of the fruit of the Spirit. Walking with God doesn't just result in the ability to wait well. There's so much more to it than that. Patience is the ability to put up with a lot for a long time and still be okay. It's stamina. Fortitude. Moxie. Endurance. Perseverance. Determination. It's not just sitting idly while not losing your temper. We use the word "patience" as a synonym for "timidity," while in the Bible it's more like "tenacity." Patience is as much about grit and guts as it is about calm and composure. Though the Greek word *makrothymia* is often translated "patience," I prefer it rendered (as it sometimes is) as "forbearance" or "long-suffering." These words have a connotation of relentlessness that can get lost in our English word "patience."

Forbearance is not a virtue that just develops our skills to politely stand by, exhibiting well-mannered inaction. It's what keeps us from giving up when things get tough. It's grit. It's the willful strength to keep going. If patience is only the ability to wait, then it's just a polite version of passivity, a hushed and considerate inactivity. Patience would then consist only of not being annoying, not raging out of control, and not speaking before being asked. It would be only about muting desires and delaying gratification. It would be the fruit of good manners. Praise the Lord that there is so much more to patience than just an idle tolerance. When parents walk by the Spirit, that shapes them into people who endure, people who are increasingly imperturbable and indefatigable.

A few years ago, I hiked up a mountain with a group of men from my church. On our last morning, as we approached the summit after days of carrying our heavy packs through the woods up endless switchbacks, we faced a series of false peaks. It would look like the summit was just over the next ridge, but then we'd get over the ridge and see we had a lot farther to go. After a handful of those, I found myself discouraged.

Patience in that circumstance didn't look like waiting for the summit to come to me. It was the strength and will to keep climbing, the willful determination to press on regardless of adversity. When my wife and I have a single friend who desires to be married, we call on him or her to be patient, but that doesn't mean waiting until God drops a spouse off on the front porch. It might involve some work to actively seek a godly mate. When I help young men discern whether they are called to be pastors, I encourage them to be patient, but that doesn't mean leaving their current employer and sitting at home waiting to see if God miraculously sends them a job offer. It involves laborious study and practice. That kind of tenacity is long-suffering patience.

Forbearance has as much to do with the ability to keep working as it does to keep waiting. Impatience is as much about giving up and quitting as it is about losing your temper. The ability to keep laboring, undaunted, despite resistance—that's patience. It's being able to put up with a lot. Long-suffering is enduring even through prolonged difficulty. The outcome of your faith in Christ is resilience and steadfastness. The result of walking with God is the strength to move forward, poised and composed, even when your circumstances are difficult. The Spirit gives you strength to keep going when you'd otherwise grow weary and collapse. This is the true relief that parents need.

In 1 Thessalonians 5:14, Paul urges Christians to "admonish the idle, encourage the fainthearted, help the weak, be patient with them all." Let's now look more closely at each part of this verse to help us more deeply understand patience. Some of what I have to say will be for the idle parent who needs to be challenged. Some will be for the fainthearted or weak parent who needs encouragement and help. You may resonate with one place more than the other, but I believe you will find some of yourself in both.

Exhausted or Lazy?

Sometimes my eyes try to remind me that I'm overdoing something. When I'm overworked and underrested, my left eyelid will twitch. When I'm worn out, I will grow bags under my eyes, and they will get blood-shot. My head will swim and ache. These are physical reminders that I'm not okay. I need to slow down, wind down, lie down, and shut down.

I know what it is to have a tired body. It's common for me to be sore by the end of the day (and at my age, often I'm sore from the climb out of bed in the morning). I know what it is to have a tired mind too. I've had days when my concentration was slipping, when I felt as though I were all out of ideas, or when my mind was dulled from a lack of sleep. Parenting, work, household chores—these can truly run me out of gas. I know that exhaustion is real. Fatigue is not a fantasy. I know what it's like to be running on empty, to not be able to keep my eyes open, to feel as if I can't keep going. To remedy genuine, sincere exhaustion, God has given us the gift of rest. For a short time, we do less so that in the long run we can do more.

Sleep is not sloth; it is a gift from God. In the right proportion to being awake, it is never lazy. Taking a break in right proportion to our labors is not a violation of God's law; it is one of his commands. One of the Ten Commandments is an imperative to take periodic breaks in order to rest. We can enjoy food and drink and friendship. We can celebrate holidays. We can go on vacation. Christian parents can rest guilt-free and grateful. Since we are finite beings who get worn down, these are all gifts from God for his people.

Yet I must confess that sometimes I don't lead my family as God has called and empowered me to, not because I'm incapable or uninformed, drained or worn out, but because I don't feel like it. I don't lack energy; I lack enthusiasm. I know God has the strength I need to keep going, and I know what he's asked me to do, but I shirk my duties anyway.

I have grown to see that often what parents call exhaustion is, in reality, a lack of desire. We don't do what we could do not because we lack the strength but because we lack the drive. We don't lack the stamina but rather the will. We simply don't want to do it. We say that we didn't lead our family spiritually, play a game with our kids, or have a real conversation with our spouse because it's "been a long day" or "a long week" or "a hard season," but in reality, we know that it's because we would rather relax than labor. Parents tell me they disciple "as they go," and by that what they mean is that seldom if ever do they put significant effort into spiritually leading their families. They say they are "too tired" to cook a meal or help with homework or initiate a hard conversation, and what they really mean is that they would rather do something else. If we are being honest, many of us could do more than we are doing.

It's certainly true that sometimes we have such a hard day that it impairs our ability to fulfill our responsibilities, but sometimes, let's be honest, that's an excuse. We know we should engage our kids with God's word. We know we should initiate a conversation instead of sinking into the sofa. We know we should interact instead of withdrawing. We know it wouldn't be that hard. We know we still have gas in the tank. We have to be vulnerable and admit that if we simply wanted to do it badly enough, it would be done—and done with excellence.

For real body and mind exhaustion, we can get relief by resting. For the lack of desire that we *call* exhaustion, we need relief in the form of gritty patience. Resilience. Forbearance. The fruit of long-suffering blesses us by helping us not tire of fulfilling our calling. We sometimes lack the perspective and motivation, but in Christ, we can find the strength needed to press on. Ask God for the patience and grit as well as the energy. Pray with me now: "Lord, help me want to do what I can even when I don't feel like it, to press forward no matter what for the sake of your kingdom under my roof! Help me endure."

Resting While Running

Several years ago I ran my first—and last—half marathon. I'm still sore. But I've been told that if you are a long-distance runner, you will sometimes "hit a wall," meaning you will reach a point in your race where you feel as if you can't go on. I hit my wall about one hundred yards into my thirteen-mile race. I've also been told that if you push through that "wall" moment and keep going, then you will experience the euphoric runner's high, an exercise-induced bliss. That sounds great, but I'm pretty skeptical about it since it's evaded me thus far every single time I've done a long-distance run (technically one single time, but that's 100 percent). As an avid eater, however, I think I can empathize. I've been at meals where I hit a wall. I felt as if I couldn't eat any more. I was stuffed. Then someone offered dessert. When I pushed through to have the cake, cookies, pie, or ice cream, I experienced a kind of eater's high. Maybe the runner's high is sort of like that.

It's not uncommon for us to hit a wall in parenting, to reach a moment when we feel as though we can't keep going. No matter how many times we ask our kids to obey, they keep doing the opposite. On top of that, we make the same mistakes over and over again. We feel the desperate need to change our pace, refuel, or even stop altogether. Pushing through might be an option or a necessity in some circumstances, but our God is so kind to us that he speaks directly to us in those moments and offers us the relief he knows we need.

In Psalm 127:2, God reminds us that it is not only okay to lie down and sleep but also a gift to those he loves. He says, "It is in vain that you rise up early and go late to rest, eating the bread of anxious toil; for he gives to his beloved sleep." Sleep is the blessed refreshment that every person needs, and it is a reminder that you are not God. Unlike you, the God who "keeps you will not slumber" (Ps. 121:3). You can trust him with the world and the details of your life.

And there's more. Sleep isn't all he offers the exhausted. In Matthew 11:28–30, Jesus bids us to come to him when we are overworked and overburdened. He says, "I will give you rest." What a treasure! The three sweetest words you could ever hear when you are tired out—"Come to me." God invites the overwhelmed to do something very simple: When I am weary, when I've hit a wall, when I'm exhausted, I am not only allowed but invited to come to Jesus. I turn to him in prayer, and I drop what is too heavy for me, knowing that he is strong enough to carry it. One of the ways we go to Jesus is by turning to the body of Christ. Go to the church with what is overwhelming you, and ask them to help "bear [your] burdens, and so fulfill the law of Christ" (Gal. 6:2). One of the most refreshing practices you can do is be an active part of what your church is doing as they gather and scatter to honor God every week.

Consider what God says through the prophet Isaiah:

Have you not known? Have you not heard?
The LORD is the everlasting God,
    the Creator of the ends of the earth.
He does not faint or grow weary;
    his understanding is unsearchable.
He gives power to the faint,
    and to him who has no might he increases strength.
Even youths shall faint and be weary,
    and young men shall fall exhausted;

but they who wait for the LORD shall renew their strength;
>   they shall mount up with wings like eagles;
> they shall run and not be weary;
>   they shall walk and not faint. (Isa. 40:28–31)

God doesn't ever get tired. And your indefatigable God offers power to the faint and weak. He renews and increases your strength not in self-confidence or self-sufficiency but in his strength. You can keep going because though you would be overwhelmed on your own, the God who empowers you never will be.

On the surface, Matthew 11 and Isaiah 40 may appear to contradict each other. You might ask, If I'm exhausted, does God want me to rest or to run? If I am following God in my house, will we get rest, or will we run and not need rest?

Yet these passages seem contradictory only because we misunderstand rest. We tend to think of rest only as relaxation. I instinctively picture rest as lying motionless on a reclining chair or swaying gently on a hammock. But in Matthew 11, Jesus doesn't paint a picture of people with nothing to do because they follow Jesus. Rather, he paints a picture of people doing work. The true rest that Jesus offers does not come from the fact that there's nothing to do or from him completing your earthly work for you. The rest you are offered comes from doing the work Christ gives you, a work that is manageable, not oppressive, because he is a good Master. He bids you to come to do this work and says that it will not be too much for you. Come to Jesus, and you will change the weight you bear, the pace you work at, and the expectations you carry for self-sufficiency.

You will rest, and you will run. In some ways, you will rest while you run. Your pace will match your strength. God is patient with you. He is never in a rush, and he is never exhausted. He can forbear in any circumstance. The fruit of doing work given to you by God will be that you too will be able to endure. When you parent in Christ, you are more than just you—you're much more. The Spirit of God is in you. Though you're a sinner, in Christ you are a victor. A liberated captive. A conqueror.

Our Long-Suffering God

If instead of feeling tired from striving, you have found yourself idle in your parenting, pray for forbearance. In Christ, you will find the way to go and the strength to get there.

Since we know we are not perfect, we expect to fall short. We anticipate a million missteps and know that we will take a million more without noticing them. As Christian parents, we should be undaunted not because we never expect to fail but because we have faith that even in every failure, mistake, and grief, God is working out a greater triumph. Part of that triumph is gained through the strength he builds in us that is learned only in the school of hard knocks. So keep going.

Right now, pause from reading this book, and go do whatever parenting work that you've been putting off. Play with your kids. Read the Bible with your family. Get up and go.

God is patient with you. That doesn't just mean that God isn't displeased with you; it means that he endures with you as he gives you the strength to endure as well. God endures our wandering from his righteousness. God endures our accusations. God endures when we are too weak.

Have you ever endured something with your children that was too hard for them to endure on their own? Have you ever had to endure when your kids did things they should not have done? Have you suffered with them when they were suffering? Have you been strong for them when they were weak? Have you ever stayed up after they went to bed to take care of their needs? How much more does God endure with you? How much more is he able to be your strength when you are weak? How much more does he take care of you while you get the sleep you need? He is not begrudging, not resistant, and not disappointed, but eager to bless and strengthen.

If God is patient with us and the fruit of walking with him is also patience, then is it any wonder that he would command us through the apostle Paul, "Let us not grow weary of doing good, for in due season we will reap, if we do not give up" (Gal. 6:9)? Let's keep going, parents! Sleep when you need sleep. Run when you're able. Pace yourself with God, who renews and increases your strength, and don't give up. Give it all you've got, resting in his sweet grace.

Resting Through Spiritual Disciplines

One last word before we wrap up this chapter. Yes, sometimes it is rest that will strengthen you when you are exhausted. But sometimes what you need more than rest is fuel. What makes a fire blaze? It's not letting the fire relax but adding wood, coal, or gasoline. To be the mom or dad you're called to be, you will need to relax sometimes, but other times you will need fuel. For parenting in Christ, you'll need fuel in the form of inspiration. Fuel in the form of spiritual growth. Fuel in the form of prayer. Fuel in the form of discipleship, accountability, and help from a wiser, more experienced parent. You will regularly need to fuel the parenting work you're doing in order to stay engaged.

The renewal and relief you need are in the billows of the Spirit. Second Timothy 1:6–7 says, "I remind you to fan into flame the gift of God, which is in you through the laying on of my hands, for God gave us a spirit not of fear but of power and love and self-control."

Refreshing practices that honor God are a gift from God himself and a beautiful part of how he restores the strength of his people. Our God is a God of holidays and feasts and festivals as well as quiet meditations and intimate relationships. He is the God who works hard and then models rest from work for us. He gives to his beloved sleep and rest. He invites his people to "eat and drink and be joyful" (Eccl. 8:15).

What do you do or stop doing to find refreshment? What do you play? What do you read? Whom do you spend time with? Where are you quiet? Where are you known? What do you like to look at? What are you passionate about? What do you love to learn about? What do you drink or eat that brings you joy? How do you take a break?

Maybe we could learn from our children on this point. Most of our kids wake up without a care in the world because they know that their mom and dad have carried all the burdens of the day for them. They play without regard for the clock. They make new friends easily, and they love their old friends effortlessly. They are carefree.

In order to be as carefree as a child while still being responsible with our calling's tasks, we will have to commit to finding refreshment. Refreshing practices may require you to carve some time out of your schedule. You may have to say no to something that seems important. You may have to complete your task list at a slower pace. You may have to put fewer activities on your calendar or space them out more. You may have to be patient with yourself.

Right now, reflect on your longing for rest and fuel. Feel it in your body, your mind, and your soul. Take a moment and grab something to eat or drink. Sit down. Close your eyes. Savor that first bite or sip. Consider how good it is to be refreshed and refueled. Take another bite or another sip. Breathe deep. Release the tension in your neck and shoulders. Open the word of God to Matthew 11:28. Hear Jesus say, "I will give you rest." Slowly read it over and over, and each time emphasize a different word in the verse.

"*I* will give you rest."

"I *will* give you rest."

"I will *give* you rest."

"I will give *you* rest."

"I will give you *rest*."

Let this passage soak into your soul for a minute. Close your eyes and savor the gift of God's patience and perseverance.

A Prayer for Energy and Enthusiasm

Heavenly Father, my reserves are depleted. I'm low on energy, and I'm responding poorly to my family's needs. Give me strength, Lord. Help me endure.

When I do get to lie down, please give me uninterrupted, sweet rest. Help me wake up refreshed. When I get a moment to myself, help me spend it wisely. Let me savor your word.

I ask that you also help me recognize when I am not too tired to do what I should and give me an enthusiasm for obedience to your will. Let me not grow weary of doing good. Give me grit and tenacity for leading the home you've given me and dealing with the situations you've led me to. When I am weak, please be strong. I confess that I need you. I depend on you. Help me soak in your sturdiness. Amen.

Reflection Questions

1. How is your energy level today?

2. What comes to mind when you hear the word "patience"?

3. How do your mind and body tell you that you are exhausted?

4. Where do you have energy but lack enthusiasm for leading your family?

5. What refreshes you?

6. How would you like to see your patience bless your children?

O, why so heavy, O my soul?
Thus to myself I said;
O, why so heavy, O my soul,
And so disquieted?

Hope thou in God; He still shall be
Thy glory and thy praise;
His saving grace shall comfort thee
Through everlasting days.

His goodness made thee what thou art,
And yet will thee redeem:
O, be thou of a steadfast heart,
And put thy trust in Him.

EDWARD CASWALL
"O, Why So Heavy, O My Soul" (1873)

7

Kindness

Relief from Bitterness

ARE YOU DOING THE MOST work in your family? As a parent, sometimes it can feel that way. You cleaned up after yourself and everyone else. You ran all the errands. You stayed up later. You got up earlier. You worked harder. You accomplished more. If we were keeping score, you'd be way ahead. It feels unfair. You're undercompensated and underappreciated. If you dwell on how much you're doing compared to others, you become hypersensitive to the slightest slight. You are easily provoked.

Are you getting the least from your family? As a parent, sometimes it can feel that way. Everyone else got a full night's sleep. Everyone else got to have fun while you worked. Everyone else enjoyed the fruits of your labor but you. You didn't get a break. You didn't get to go out. You didn't get to stay in. You didn't get what you wanted so that everyone else could get what they wanted. If we were keeping score, you'd be way behind. It feels unfair. You're undercompensated and underappreciated. If you dwell on what you're not getting compared to others, you become hypersensitive to the slightest slight. You are easily provoked.

Comparisons like these foster the poison of bitterness, but it can be relieved by the gift of God's kindness. God is doing way more than we are, and yet his heart toward us is not bitter or spiteful. If we could follow his example and be a source of sincere kindness, we would experience relief from anguish over how much we are getting or doing.

An Act of Kindness or an Act of Credit?

It can be fun to do kind things for your family. Sometimes I'll even invite my kids to do acts of kindness with me. On one such occasion, I took one of them along to buy an anniversary present for Mom. We picked out a great steel coffee mug for her and paid to get it personalized. I asked my son what he thought we should put on it that would bless her. Without hesitation (and without too much thought) he said, "H-A-M. For 'Happy anniversary, Mommy.'" We treasure that HAM coffee mug to this day.

It's great to do things that will delight the ones you love. But honestly, I have frequently fought the temptation to be kind in order to get something in return. I am often tempted to try to be caught doing what I'm supposed to do. There's a desire in my heart to be appreciated and approved, and that itch gets scratched only if my work or generosity is noticed. It would be prideful to say, "Hey! Did you see the awesome things I did?" But it seems humble to get "caught" in the act of doing dishes or vacuuming or taking out the trash.

I don't just want to clean our house; I want my children and my wife to know and appreciate that I cleaned the house. What good is it if they don't see me doing it and applaud me for it? I don't just want to assemble a new piece of furniture and do the laundry and fix the plumbing; I want my children and my wife to notice and appreciate that I did all that.

If no one mentions my efforts, I can even feel slighted and hurt. I want to be repaid for my efforts with, at the very least, gratitude and acknowledgment. If I feel as if my accomplishments or contributions go unnoticed, I might even find subtle (or not-so-subtle) ways to draw attention to them. This converts what would otherwise be acts of kindness into acts of credit. Any lack of credit where I believe credit is due can develop in me self-pity and even animosity toward others. When I don't get recognition, I become resentful—even in small things. And that makes me bitter; I carry around a sour, self-inflicted pain that makes it seem as if it's someone else's fault that I feel antagonistic.

Even worse than going unnoticed is being criticized or accused. If I cleaned but "missed a spot," if I got the groceries but "forgot one item," if I changed the oil but neglected to "fill up the gas tank," or if I picked up all the toys but "put something away in the wrong place," you'll probably see me get flustered. Even if my critics are right, their words feel like an injustice to me. In the court system of my mind, labor should insulate me from critique. When instead of "Thank you!" or "Great work!" I hear "What about this?" I feel wronged. And when I feel I've been wronged, my heart's response is often not what it should be.

When we feel as if we should get something that we are not receiving, it is all too easy for us to grow a sense of resentment and bitterness, even if small. Bitterness is unforgiveness that results from holding onto a grudge against someone for not giving us what we believe we deserve. We don't typically see it or acknowledge it, but it often reveals itself when we become passive-aggressive, use cutting sarcasm, lash out, or do something out of spite. On the other hand, sometimes it can make us withdraw, isolate, and pout. Not getting what we want hurts our feelings.

While there are definitely situations when we are not being seen or cared for well by our families and it should be addressed in a godly manner, the bitterness that I'm talking about is a result of sinful entitlement or even just a sinful response to an accidental hurt done to us. Bitter entitlement whispers in our mind that we are doing more than others or that we are in a higher position over others. Something tells us we deserve better than we are receiving, so we operate out of hurt, which makes things worse for us and also potentially hurts others.

In parenting there is no shortage of opportunity for bitter entitlement. For those of us who are parenting with a spouse, the scales seldom balance perfectly. Further, parents are in authority over younger people who feel entitled to acts of service. Kids do not always know how to show deference, gratitude, and respect. Thus, the daily grind of parenting is accomplishing difficult, thankless tasks for people who perpetuate the needs rather than help meet them. It's a petri dish for resentment, the perfect environment to develop bitterness toward a spouse or a child.

Such hardworking parents would do well to heed what Christ preaches in the Sermon on the Mount about "practicing your righteousness before other people in order to be seen by them" (Matt. 6:1). The reason we serve our families is not to earn some credit, and our labors do not create a debt that is owed to us. Rather, we serve our families in order to honor them and God. Walking with God will breed a desire to do that without regard to whether we are praised for it or treated kindly in return. Being in step with the Spirit will lead to kindness that does not need acknowledgment or compensation.

Parenting is, by nature, lopsided work. We labor disproportionately to the other members of our family. So will you do that work as acts of credit, letting bitterness seep into your heart? Or will you do your uneven and unappreciated tasks out of the kindness that comes from walking by the Spirit?

Unlike an act of credit, an act of kindness does not tempt you to become bitter over how others respond to your service. You can be free from an unhappy sense of injustice by being kind. To be free of bitterness, all you have to do is labor while "count[ing] others more significant than yoursel[f]"—or, in other words, with the attitude of Christ (Phil. 2:3; cf. 2:5). It's when we think of ourselves more highly than we ought (Rom. 12:3) that resentment poisons our family relationships and twists our expectations about what we're owed.

I wish that the reason I serve my family could always be sincere kindness. It's sickening to consider how often my best efforts are acts of credit, keeping score of who is doing more or getting less. I need to run to Jesus and drop these practices at his feet.

What Does the Title Entitle You To?

When my boys were little, they loved to invent superheroes. A superhero almost always has a name or title that gives you a clue about what powers they have. One of my sons once asked me to draw a picture of the hero he'd imagined—Tiger Man. Naturally, I asked for some tips on how to draw him. According to my son, Tiger Man has the body of a tiger and the head of—pause for effect—a tiger.

You have a powerful title. You are Dad or Mom, which is an imposing designation to your child. You are in a position of authority. Jesus says that people who don't follow God will use their position and power to lord it over those they lead. As moms and dads, we feel the prerogative to do what we want since we're in a position of authority. I admit that I often talk to my own kids in ways that I would never talk to someone else. I speak disrespectfully because, in my mind, my position entitles me to their respect. I feel entitled to their obedience and bitter when I don't get it. I am even entitled to their forgiveness when I mess up. I am often kinder to strangers than I am to my own kids. With strangers, I don't know what they think of me, and I don't care. With my kids, I expect their love and loyalty. It's owed. I demand it, so my kindness diminishes.

The scary reality is that there are very effective ways to get your family to do what you want that don't come from walking by the Spirit. You can get your family to do what you want by threatening them, thus acting as an entitled tyrant. You can also lead your family by bribing them, thus relinquishing your authority to your children. Both methods can foster more bitterness as you look at your family and despise "who they make you become." I do believe that parents should discipline disobedience and reward obedience, but that is different from leading a house in a way that manipulates behavior through fear or bartering.

Unlike such manipulation tactics, when you walk with the Spirit, you can lead your family with kindness. Other people may use their authority to rule and force compliance, but Jesus says, "It shall not be so among you" (Matt. 20:26). To be the greatest dad or the greatest mom, you must become the servant of all, letting go of the entitlement that has been leading you all astray. What does having the title of "Dad" entitle you to? Honor? Yes. Your children should honor you. But your title does not make you an authority who is excused from serving and deserves to be served.

In the church I pastor, when a man becomes an elder, he receives a challenge coin. This tradition comes from the military and police. When a member joins one of these groups or goes on a particular mission, he is given a challenge coin to commemorate the event. For our elders, their coin is a reminder to be in prayer for the people they are overseeing and shepherding. On that coin is the Latin phrase *Praesis ut prosis ne ut imperes*, which means "Lead in order to serve, not in order to rule." That is also what it means for us to lead as parents. In order to lead, we serve—even if the ones we serve have not earned it.

You are a mother or a father, but you would do well to remember that your children are just that—still children. Why is it so shocking to me when my kids act like kids? Because they don't want what I want. Or they are not doing what I want them to do. Of course they don't, and of course they are not! They are children. They are still relatively new to Earth.

Bitter entitlement says to a child who is not meeting my expectations, "How dare you!" A heart filled with kindness is able to say, "You didn't meet my expectations because there was something you wanted more than honoring me. That is a hard choice for all of us." A kind heart is not offended by the disobedience of a child; it helps them see what they should want and what they should do. It does not want retribution; it wants repair and restoration.

No one likes a sense of entitlement in kids, but it's even less appealing in parents. It's just harder for us to see in ourselves. Bitterly entitled parents are keeping a tally. They look at all they are doing, and they believe they deserve better. If someone under them has cheated them out of their rightful due, then look out.

The way to overcome bitter entitlement is to recognize yourself not as a person to whom people owe a debt but as a person who has experienced the incredible forgiveness of debt in Christ. Because of the kindness of God to you, be eager to see that kindness overflow from you to others. Because of what you've been given, delight to bless others, whether they see such blessing or not.

In the Sermon on the Mount, Jesus tells us to "sound no trumpet" about our acts of kindness (Matt. 6:2). We can be so free in Christ that we can be kind and serve even if no one notices and not be unsettled by that. In fact, Jesus encourages us to do acts of kindness in secret, knowing that our "Father who sees in secret will reward [us]" (Matt. 6:4). If you want to tip the scales in your favor, don't make it about getting more approval and appreciation—that is the path to bitterness. Instead, strive to "outdo one another in showing honor" (Rom. 12:10) because when we walk by the Spirit, we will delight to be kind without regard to earthly rewards.

Weeping over Those Who Rejoice

One of the clearest indicators that a parent's heart is not fully set free is an inability to sincerely celebrate something good happening to someone else. When someone else's vacation stories or pictures make me feel bad, I know something is wrong with me. When envy is my response to a young child demonstrating more maturity, talent, or brilliance than my child, then I know something is off. When someone else's mother-daughter activity or father-son trip makes me feel self-conscious, I know I need Jesus to free me from whatever is going on in my mind.

If someone else's spouse, house, or kids sparks jealousy in my heart, then my heart is not free. Resenting someone else's progress or prosperity comes from bitterness. True freedom wouldn't twist what they have into an indictment over what I don't.

In Romans 12:15, Paul tells us to "rejoice with those who rejoice, weep with those who weep." But I see a very common temptation in parents to weep when others have something to rejoice over and to rejoice when they are not the ones weeping. Something in us is not okay. We need relief from this.

Freedom from bitterness would let me not only rejoice with those who rejoice but even feel honored and delighted to celebrate a blessing, whether it blessed me personally or not. When we recognize that we are truly free in Christ, then good anywhere for anyone will cause us to cheer.

What About Me?

When someone else gets something that a child wants, he is quick to point out that it's not "fair." To him, "fair" means everyone getting the same thing. I've told my children many times that if we are going to use that flawed definition, then we'll need to shave all their heads (including Mom's) because it's not "fair" that I'm the only bald one in the family. At the root of most bitterness is a form of self-pity or a perceived unfairness.

We see exactly that in Luke 15, where Jesus tells three stories about finding lost things—a sheep, a coin, and a son. Each story concludes with an invitation to celebrate with the one who got back what he or she loved. In the third story, the lost son rebels against his father and runs away to squander his inheritance on reckless living. When he returns, his father celebrates and throws a party. At the end of the story, Jesus tells us that the lost son had an older brother who heard about the celebration and refused to join. He was so bitter that the party was for his little brother even though he felt as if he (the older brother) and his friends deserved it more. Something in his heart wouldn't let him celebrate something good for his brother. It wasn't fair.

This is a struggle for all human hearts. Something good for someone else leaves us asking, Why not me? It's a question you rarely hear anyone ask when someone gets bad news.

For example, in John 21:18–22, Jesus tells Peter that when Peter is older, he'll be taken somewhere he does not want to go, and his death will not be pretty. And Peter does what our hearts love to do when we get a bad prognosis. He looks behind him, points to John, and asks Jesus, "What about him?" Jesus answers by clarifying that Peter's call is to follow him, not to be concerned about what that calling looks like for different people.

A person whose heart is set free by God will walk in kindness even when things don't seem fair. We don't all get dealt the same hand in life. And we don't always get what we want. But in Christ, we have everything we need. This provision of the Spirit lets us be free to sincerely revel in others' successes and grieve over their losses. We can gladly serve without compensation and without acknowledgment.

Even when we have been truly wronged, we can forgive as we have been forgiven. Christian forgiveness uproots the bitterness in our hearts. The kindness we have received from God inoculates us against spite. The kindness we show others because of God's love, if we offer it sincerely, cannot coexist with grudges and malice. Walking with our kind God increases kindness in our hearts. And true kindness delivers relief to a parent who would otherwise be vindictive.

What is something kind that you could do right now without anyone noticing? The bigger the better. Put down the book for a minute, and see if you can honor someone and get away with it. Consecrate this act as an offering to God. Feel how that satisfies your heart.

A Prayer for Times of Bitterness

Heavenly Father, I am having trouble forgiving others. I've been hurt. I feel wronged. I feel unseen, unheard, and unappreciated. I know how much forgiveness you have given me. Give me that same heart toward others.

I know I have counted my efforts and tallied others' shortcomings. I have compared my best to their worst. Something in my heart feels unsettled. Please relieve me of this burden of bitterness. Give me a heart of kindness. Show me how to be generous. Teach me to rejoice with those who rejoice and to weep with those who weep. Amen.

Reflection Questions

1. Do you keep score in your home? Where are you behind or ahead?

2. Have you ever resented someone else's achievements or success and felt insecure as a result?

3. Where do you see God's kindness in your life?

4. What does God's forgiveness mean to you?

5. What is a creative way that you could serve your family without seeking acknowledgment?

6. How do you feel when you consider getting no credit for serving?

No more, my God, I boast no more,
Of all the duties I have done:
I quit the hopes I held before
To trust the merits of thy Son.

Now for the love I bear his name,
What was my gain I count my loss:
My former pride I call my shame,
And nail my glory to his cross.

Yes, and I must and will esteem
All things but loss for Jesus' sake:
Oh, may my soul be found in him,
And of his righteousness partake!

The best obedience of my hands
Dares not appear before thy throne;
But faith can answer thy demands
By pleading what my Lord has done.

ISAAC WATTS
"The Value of Christ and His Righteousness" (1707)

8

Goodness

Relief from Inadequacy

ALLOW ME TO START this chapter with some blunt honesty: I wrestle with a consistent sense of inadequacy. It's true. I'd like to say it's humble awareness of my own shortcomings. And maybe it is sometimes. But often what I struggle with is a self-centered brand of insecurity. There is an egotistical grief in me over not being greater than I am. Call it impostor syndrome. Call it self-doubt. Call it persistent feelings of failure. Whatever you call it, I tend to believe that I will inevitably disappoint others, and that disappoints me.

As a pastor who sees himself as inadequate, I charge my church to follow God in areas where I fail, and sometimes I shove that in my own face. As a father who sees himself as inadequate, I charge my sons to follow God in ways that I fall obviously short, and I beat myself up about it. Sometimes it crosses my mind that they deserve someone better than me to parent them.

I have no problem believing criticism, and I shrug off encouragements. I speak to myself in ways I'd never let someone else speak to me. I advise others to be reassured in ways I struggle to be reassured myself. Perhaps you can relate.

Inadequacy seems like the truest thing about me. Those who know me may call it "being hard on myself" or even "delusional," but to me it feels as if I'm just self-aware. I feel a persistent, nagging sense that my best is not good enough or that I'm not doing enough good. I can always offer an apology because I could always do more and could always do better. I worry about what people think of me because I know I have glaring flaws and weaknesses. I have a stubborn fear of man—I'm always looking around at people to see if I'm doing okay. I even worry about what God thinks of me. I want to hear him say, "Well done, good and faithful servant" (Matt. 25:23). But I look at my life and think it's likely I might hear him say, "Why didn't you do more with what I gave you?"

One of my favorite pastors from the nineteenth century, Charles Spurgeon, called this "an overwhelming sense of [one's] own unworthiness."[1] I see my incompetence, and I am painfully aware of my unfitness and my shortcomings. Where does my humble understanding of not being perfect stop, and where does prideful self-insult begin?

I write this chapter with a heart that needs to hear and believe the very things I want to share with you. I am not writing from a place of strength. I am speaking from a heart that needs relief.

I know that I am walking with the Spirit, but sometimes it's hard to believe that goodness is something that is coming out of me as a result. Of course, I do believe that all people fall short of the glory of God and are therefore inadequate, but that belief sometimes leads to a pessimism about any goodness in me, even as fruit from the Spirit.

Feeling Underdressed

One time after phys ed in fifth grade, my classmates and I were in the locker room changing out of our gym clothes and back into our school clothes when a shockingly loud tornado siren went off. Our teacher

---

1   Charles Haddon Spurgeon, "Zechariah's Vision of Joshua the High Priest," in *Metropolitan Tabernacle Pulpit* (London, 1865), 11:51.

came crashing through the locker room door in a panic and rushed us into the back of the shower room. It turns out that the shower rooms were the school's tornado shelter, so the teachers also began to usher the rest of the school in there with us. And it wasn't a drill. We were in that shower room for over an hour. I ended up sitting right next to a group of eighth-grade girls. Proximity to these mature young ladies would have been enough to make me feel uneasy and self-conscious for that cruel hour, but the worst part of the whole experience was that I never had the time to get fully dressed when the alarm went off. I sat in the corner of that locker room only half dressed for what felt like eternity. My pale chest, scrawny arms, and countable ribs were on full display to the crowd of glancing, snickering eighth-grade beauties. I had never felt more exposed and embarrassed. I considered whether it might be better just to run out of the door and be carried away by the twister.

In Zechariah 3, the prophet describes a vision he had of the high priest, Joshua, standing in front of God in filthy clothes. Satan stood to Joshua's right, ready to accuse him. The high priest was supposed to serve God in pure, clean white linen, so Joshua was way out of line. His iniquity had disqualified him from standing in the presence of God. It was obvious—he was underdressed and unworthy.

I have no trouble imagining what it feels like to be lacking in such a physically obvious way. It is uncomfortable. You feel exposed, grossly self-conscious, like a failure or a disappointment. When you are under-dressed and inadequate, anyone's gaze is unnerving, let alone that of someone you admire or want to impress.

In Zechariah's vision, Satan stands ready to accuse Joshua, presum-ably about his unfitness to serve God. Joshua is supposed to lead the people in following Yahweh, and he's clearly unfit. If you were to stand before God to be evaluated as a mom or dad, how would it go? Would you feel unworthy? If your family's opponent, Satan, was standing nearby to accuse you, what would he say? Think of how easily the list of accusations could come: "I've seen them be so lazy! I've got count-less examples of them being inattentive. I've heard them be harsh and impatient. Want to know about their persistent selfishness? Pick a day, and I'll give you an example! Want to see them be callous toward these kids they claim to love? It's shameful."

We make Satan's job easy. We are woefully guilty. Our unworthiness to lead the children God gave us is all too obvious. If our garments represented our parenting, they'd be filthy. To stand before God and give an account of our household like that would be uncomfortable. It would be truly heartbreaking. We are all lacking.

Yet in Zechariah's vision, Satan is quickly rebuked by God. He is silenced. But God doesn't argue that Joshua is innocent or sufficient. He doesn't say, "Joshua is good enough for me! He may not meet your standard, Satan, but he meets mine!" It is not the work of Joshua that makes him suddenly fit. Interestingly, it is not any inaccuracy of Satan's accusations either. Rather, it is the work of God that makes Joshua acceptable without any argument over Joshua's guilt. Joshua is described as one "plucked" by God from the fire (3:2). God knows Joshua's shortcomings, and he overcomes them. God cleanses Joshua's sin. God changes his clothes and, by extension, Joshua's fitness for the calling on his life.

Consider this: there is nothing that Satan (or anyone else for that matter) could accuse you of that God is not aware of already. There's no secret corner of your inadequacy that God has not explored. God is not ignorant. Neither does he ignore sin. He doesn't pretend to not notice the filthy garments on Joshua but rather replaces them. God does not overlook sin but overcomes it in the life of the believer. God does not pretend that our debts don't exist but pays for them by the blood of Christ. Thus, Christian parents do not have to wallow in shame or hide from their mistakes but can be confident in the cleansing work of God to make them fit for the calling he has given them. They walk free because their incalculable debt is paid in full.

An Accurate Accuser and an Adoring Advocate

I fully believe in this grace. I believe it applies to me. I believe that I am saved and that I did not merit it. But I struggle with the fact that the accusations of the enemy are so accurate. John tells us in Revelation 12:10 that he heard a voice in heaven describe Satan as "the accuser of our brothers" who "accuses them day and night before our God." We have an accuser, and sadly, our inadequacy is obvious. There's plenty of ammunition. This is part of where my struggle lies. In his brilliance, Satan doesn't always use lies to deceive us or accuse us. The accuser makes some good points. He's not always wrong.

Yet even when he points out the truth, he is actually twisting the truth into something that drives me away from God. Jesus, on the other hand, draws a picture of sin as something that should drive me into the loving arms of God like a beloved child who knows he has made a terrible mistake but also knows he's still loved by his father.

Satan, God, and I all know that I'm far from perfect. But God bids me come to him and experience his compassion, while Satan makes me want to hide and withdraw. The accusations of inadequacy would have me believing that the solution, the relief, would come from me being greater than I am. That unless I got better, I would be trying to serve a disappointed God. That if I could just improve myself, I could fight off the accusations by myself and disprove the arguments about my guilt. True relief from inadequacy, however, does not come from self-improvement. If it did, all of us would always fall short. We are inadequate in overcoming our inadequacy. Thank God that true relief comes from his transformational power, love, and grace. His love is good, and it breeds goodness in me.

As Christians, we should not seek to hide sin. Rather, we should bring our own trespasses to light and lovingly address them in others. When Christians address sin in ourselves or others, it is to bring reconciliation, to restore us to God and each other. Satan does the opposite.

He wants to expose sin in order to drive a wedge between people and God. His accusations are meant to separate us and shame us. Satan wants to foster rejection, while we want to foster restoration.

In Revelation 12, John tells us about not only our accuser but also our advocate. And in 1 John 2:1, he says, "My little children, I am writing these things to you so that you may not sin. But if anyone does sin, we have an advocate with the Father, Jesus Christ the righteous." For every accusation of the accuser, there is a rebuttal from our advocate. Jesus Christ the righteous declares that his blood cleanses us from our sin. He declares that his righteousness is shared with us. He declares that his power sustains and empowers us for the good he calls us to.

That's Not Jesus

On a day when I was struggling with a sense of not being enough, my friend Jamin posed a hypothetical scenario. He asked me to imagine that my son got a note at school that said something like this:

> My dear child,
>
> I hope you are having a good day. I dropped off this note for you at school because there are just a few things I've neglected to mention to you lately, and I wanted to communicate them clearly, so I wrote them down for you.
>
> First, I know you've been struggling a lot lately. There are some very difficult circumstances you're navigating. I just want you to know that I see what you are going through, I know how hard it is, and I need you to know that your response to these challenges has been a major disappointment to me. I think my expectations for you were just too high. You have made a mess of your life, and it's become something that is reflecting poorly on me. Frankly, I'm humiliated. I can only assume you are too. You've proved yourself to be a failure and a disappointment.
>
> I wanted so much more from you. I wanted to see something so different, so much better. Your mistakes are making it really hard for

me to love and support you. I see a lot of other kids your age facing similar hardships, and it has become clear how deficient you are in comparison. The difference is glaring. I guess I expected too much from you. You have let me down.

Sincerely,

Your father

Jamin asked me how I thought my son would respond to a note like that. "I think he'd be heartbroken," I said.

Jamin said, "Maybe. But don't you think part of your son would say, 'I don't think my dad wrote this. That doesn't sound like my father'?"

My breath caught a little. I could hear the truth my friend was sharing with me, and it touched my heart. My kids know my voice. My kids know my heart. They'd know better than to believe I'd insult them and discourage them like that.

The truth is, I know my heavenly Father's voice well enough to know that the insults of incompetence I tend to believe are not coming from him. I had seen the accuracy of these accusations, and I clung to them because they rang true. I had heard the truth of unloving criticism, and I wouldn't let it go. Yet while I was imagining the disappointment of God, I had not taken the time to consider if what I was perceiving was coming from the voice of my Father or somewhere else. Would my heavenly Father really talk to me like that?

If I, an imperfect father, would never say things like that to my child, how much more can I be sure that my perfect heavenly Father would never seek to crush me by rubbing my face in my own sin and shortcomings or frown on me just because I needed him? My heavenly Father has compassion for his children. I knew that. I was just acting like I forgot it.

Jesus says about his people, "I know my own and my own know me" (John 10:14). He says that his people hear his "voice" (10:3). When

I heard insulting accusations of inadequacy, I had been struggling to see who was talking, and I was clinging to them instead of pushing them away.

I want you to consider for a minute some of the things that Jesus did and did not say during his earthly ministry. Here are just a few:

"I don't like you."
    That's not Jesus.
"Love one another as I have loved you."
    That's Jesus.

"You have nothing good to offer."
    That's not Jesus.
"If you remain in me and I in you, you will bear much fruit."
    That's Jesus.

"You're on your own."
    That's not Jesus.
"Behold, I am with you always, to the end of the age."
    That's Jesus.

"Go away from me!"
    That's not Jesus.
"Come to me."
    That's Jesus.

Take a second and consider any negative evaluations of your parenting that you are listening to right now. Of course you're not perfect; we'll address that momentarily. But are you feeling as though you have *nothing* good to offer? Are you feeling as though you need to overcome the world on your own? Are you feeling as though God is disappointed in you, and that's driving you away from him?

My Goodness

Understanding how the theology of God's pleasure applies to my work has been a long journey for me. I am so grateful for the many theological influences in my life that have shaped what I believe and the way I interpret the Scriptures. I believe, however, that a lot of what I was taught about sin and being "a polluted garment" (Isa. 64:6) has led me to a false assumption about both my worth to God and my ability to please him.

Though the Bible does not teach works righteousness—that I can be saved by my own merit—it does talk about the beauty of righteous works. Sadly, I misunderstood the latter as salvific goodness and thus ignored it. I don't know if that was ever taught to me explicitly, but it was easy to believe that God saved a "worthless" being like me. On the other hand, it was not easy to believe that he saved me because of his love for me, because of my value to him.

This has left me with an underdeveloped sense of what it looks like for a sinful dad like me to please God. I know that my children aren't perfect, and yet they please me all the time! How much more might a perfect heavenly Father be pleased with an imperfect child like me exercising faith?

I don't refrain from celebrating my children or encouraging their obedience for fear that they'll attach my pleasure and love to their achievements. I also do not withhold love from them until they achieve perfection. I am pleased with them often and sincerely, and the truth is that my love is not on the line when they disobey. As far as I can see, they run no risk of losing my love.

I believe that those of you who are in Christ, those of you with faith in God, can in fact please God. Very much so. His love for you is not fickle.

Hebrews 11:6 says that "without faith it is impossible to please him," and Romans 8:8 says that "those who are in the flesh cannot please

God." But these passages imply that those who have faith and those who are in the Spirit do, in fact, please God! You who trust Christ, you have a union with the Son of God, and you please God. You are not worthless, and you are not a constant source of displeasure to your heavenly Father.

In 1 Thessalonians 2:4, Paul says that we make great efforts to please God: "We have been approved by God to be entrusted with the gospel, so we speak, not to please man, but to please God who tests our hearts." This implies that we can be approved by God, and we can do work that pleases him.

Goodness is a fruit of the Spirit. That means that when we walk with God, our life will display goodness. Because of our relationship with God, we will do good things. We will do things that please God. We are even warned to "not neglect to do good," for that is "pleasing to God" (Heb. 13:16).

This may be uncomfortable for you to consider if you believe your identity in Christ is still the "chief of sinners" (cf. 1 Tim. 1:15). But it's not that you are good enough on your own—you have been washed clean and plucked out of the fire. The work of God, not your own work, has secured you. Now in light of God's work in your life, you can produce some goodness. You walk on a firm foundation. Goodness is fruit that comes from abiding in Christ.

This goodness is sweet relief to the heart that refuses to believe that it has anything but inadequacy to offer. Through the Spirit of God in you, there is goodness. And according to Jesus, that goodness in you will bring glory to God. He says to his followers, "Let your light shine before others, so that they may see your good works and give glory to your Father who is in heaven" (Matt. 5:16).

When your kids see goodness in you, you should not let it swell into pride, but neither should you dismiss it by focusing on your inadequacy. Attribute it to the Spirit, and by doing so, bring glory to God in your household!

"Everyone Makes Mistakes" and "Nobody's Perfect"

I wholeheartedly believe that "nobody's perfect" and that "everyone makes mistakes," but I find it confounding that these sentiments are so often expressed as a means of comfort. It's good to know that we are not alone in our imperfection, and it is good to know that mistakes are not surprising, but is that our greatest consolation?

It is absolutely "okay to not be okay." I've heard it said a hundred times in churches, and it's true. The body of Christ is a safe place to struggle. But if we lose sight of how it can also be "good to be good" or that it is "okay to be okay," then we don't have much tangible hope to offer. We shouldn't tell people, "It's okay; you'll never be okay." Rather, we have an opportunity to tell the sufferer and the struggler, "The result of walking with the Spirit will be goodness in your life, and goodness is good for you and for everyone else." Yes, we will suffer. Yes, we will struggle. But how sweet it is of God to grow goodness in our lives through our relationship with him! It's okay to be okay, and it's more than okay to stay that way.

When you sin against your kids, is it a greater comfort to say to yourself, "No parent is perfect," or, "There is forgiveness for sin, so I'll repent and pursue the beautiful goodness God talks about that comes from walking with him"? When you lose your temper, is there more gospel relief in knowing that "everyone makes mistakes" or in knowing that God cleanses us from our transgressions and calls us to something greater? When the Bible talks about the sin of all mankind, it discusses this not only to comfort us with the fact that everyone is failing but to reveal our need for God. Let that be true in your home as well. When you see your inadequacy, let it drive you toward your good God and the goodness he grows in you through his Spirit.

"You Can Do It!"

Nobody in my family gets everything right all the time. When my sons were too little to read, I asked them if they knew any of the Ten

Commandments from the Bible. One of my sons boldly recalled hearing in church that we are "not to climb adult trees" (i.e., commit adultery). Not quite, but still good advice.

In Deuteronomy, Moses gives a long speech of instruction and encouragement to a new generation of Israelites and repeats the Ten Commandments that had been given to their parents at Mount Sinai, including the command that Jesus would later call the greatest in the entire Bible—loving God with everything you've got! Right after that, Moses tells the Israelites to diligently teach their kids to love and obey God. He commands these new parents to teach the next generation about God all the time and everywhere they go.

You might be thinking, "Who can actually do all that?" And perhaps some of the Israelite parents felt the same. Yet at the end of his speech, Moses tells them that this is "not too hard" for them (30:14)! He encourages this huge crowd by saying, "You can do it" (30:11).

Of course, none of us are strong enough to perfectly follow God and raise our kids. We are all struggling and stumbling through this parenthood journey. In fact, if the quality of our parenting determined every outcome for our kids, we'd all be in big trouble. We are all imperfect parents.

But we have the help of a perfect God! We plant seeds of the gospel. We water them often. But it is God who "gives the growth" (1 Cor. 3:7)! And since God is with you, since he loves your kids, since he gives you his church to help you, since he equips you for obedience, since you can cast all your burdens on him, since you can be forgiven for your mistakes, you can do it! You can follow God and raise your kids in a way that honors him.

This is a beautiful part of our story as children of God. We are less than perfect, but we are not worthless. We are loved. We are inadequate in many ways, but we are not insignificant or inept. We are empowered and charged by the all-powerful God who promises to be with us. When you feel insecure, there is no greater promise to cling to than when Jesus says, "I am with you always" (Matt. 28:20).

God is with us as he was with Joshua the high priest. In Zechariah 3, God plucks Joshua out of the fire, rescues him from Satan's accusations, and cleanses him from his iniquity—and that isn't even the end of Joshua's story. After God cleanses him, he calls him and tells the now well-dressed high priest, "Walk in my ways" (3:7).

Yes, we are imperfect. Yes, we make mistakes. Yes, we sin. Yes, we cannot save ourselves. But when we focus on only those truths, we can get down on ourselves. Don't forget that we can serve God. We can please God. We can glorify God. Goodness is a result of walking with God, and *you are* walking with God. We are sinners, but we are not worthless. We are mistake makers, but in Christ we are not incapable of pleasing God. God calls us to please him by exercising our faith. Because you walk with the Spirit, there is goodness available to you in Christ and relief from all kinds of inadequacy.

Consider what it is to see God's goodness worked out in you. Does someone have a need you could meet right now? You are more than capable of giving a good, sincere, uplifting word that will encourage that person. Who could you bless in this way? Take a moment and send an encouragement to someone who needs it. Maybe write an encouraging note to your child or spouse. Then consider Matthew 5:16, and give glory to your Father who is in heaven for the good he does through you.

A Prayer for Times of Insecurity and Inadequacy

Heavenly Father, I have trouble seeing the good in me that comes from you. I feel unvalued and unworthy. Sometimes I lack the confidence to act on what I know to be right.

But I choose to believe that my union with your Son, Jesus Christ, has changed me and given me faith that pleases you. Use me, Lord. I surrender all my strength to you. Do good through me that will bless my family. Protect me from both pride and passivity.

Be pleased with my worship. Be pleased with my sacrifice. Be pleased with my efforts. Be glorified in the good you do through me. Amen.

Reflection Questions

1. When do you usually experience insecurity or inadequacy? How does it make you feel?

2. If a child of yours said to you, "I'm not good at anything!" how would you respond?

3. What is something that Jesus said that you want to keep at the front of your mind as you parent your kids?

4. How do you currently address sin in yourself and others?

5. What is the difference between the ways that Satan and Jesus handle your sin?

6. What are areas of your life where you would like to do more good works?

Faith to the conscience whispers peace,
And bids the mourner's sighing cease:
By faith the children's right we claim,
And call upon our Father's name.

Faith feels the Spirit's kindling breath
In love and hope that conquer death;
Faith brings us to delight in God,
And blesses e'en his smiting rod.

Such faith in us, O God, implant,
And to our prayers thy favor grant
In Jesus Christ, thy saving Son,
Who is our fount of health alone.

In him may every trusting soul
Press onward to the heavenly goal,
The blessedness no foes destroy.
Eternal love and light and joy!

PETRUS HERBERT
"Faith Is a Living Power from Heaven" (1566)

9

Faithfulness

Relief from Fear

GERMOPHOBIA IS THE FEAR of germs and dirt.

Dystychiphobia is the fear of accidents.

Sociophobia is the fear of being humiliated.

Algophobia is the fear of pain.

Atelophobia is the fear of being imperfect or making mistakes.

Catagelophobia is the fear of being mocked and criticized.

Necrophobia is the fear of death.

Theophobia is the fear of God's wrath.

Arachibutyrophobia is the fear of peanut butter sticking to the roof of your mouth.

Hippopotomonstrosesquipedaliophobia is the fear of long words.

There is no end to the list of fears we could name. And parents are no strangers to fear. We comfort our little ones when they are afraid of things real or imagined. We reassure them when they have nightmares. We leave the night-light on and close closet doors at bedtime. We hug them during storms. We protect them from danger.

As they grow, we help them overcome their fears. We encourage them to learn to swim even if (or because) they fear drowning. We teach them to ride a bike even if they're afraid of falling over. We challenge them to try new things and take risks that will help them grow and mature.

Of course, we have our own fears to navigate. As parents, we must cope with our own concerns. Most parents see a lot to fear in this world.

What is it that you fear? What situations make you feel a little panicked? Do you fear things that your kids might go through or do?

Maybe you'll relate to some of mine. There have been times when I sneak into my kids' room at night just to make sure they are still breathing while they sleep. I have triple-checked that the doors to my house are locked before I go to bed. I have expressed concern to church leaders about potential weaknesses in their child protection policies. I pray diligently on takeoffs, landings, and road trips.

Of course, while I fear for my kids' safety, I think my biggest fears are about relationships. These fears are mostly centered on potential futures and the outcomes of my parenting. I fear not having a great relationship with my kids when they grow up. I fear their resentment. I fear our family drifting apart. I fear my kids not following Jesus.

I assume I'm not the only one with these thoughts. But I want to remind you and be reminded now that dread is not a fruit of the Spirit. Walking with God does not increase the number of things that we have to fear but decreases them. Being in step with the Spirit will grow our faith, and as faith grows, fear shrinks. Faith relieves fears.

Full of Faith

Though we often translate *pistis* in Galatians 5:22 as "faithfulness," when it is used elsewhere in the New Testament, it is most often translated as "faith." In English we use the term "faithfulness" to mean trustworthiness or loyalty, but the word here in the Greek is more like the state of having faith—to be full of faith. Thus, in Galatians 5, Paul may be talking less about how walking with God will make you reliable and more about how walking with God will lead to more reliance on the Father.[1] According to Paul, walking by the Spirit will produce faith in you.

To have faith in Jesus is to trust him. It is to rely on him. Faith is the fruit of the Spirit that addresses all the struggles we've discussed so far in this book, as well as the ones we'll discuss in the remaining chapters. Faith provides a firm foundation in all circumstances.

Thus, on the flip side, it is the lack of faith that leads to our emotional burdens. What is the source of anxiety? Not trusting God with your circumstances. Why do we feel shame? We don't trust what God has declared about us. Why do we despair? We lack faith that God is still in charge and still good. Why do we feel inadequate? We don't have faith that God can cleanse us and equip us.

If our faith would increase, if we could trust God more, if we would believe he is who he says he is, that he can do what he says he can do, and that we are as valued and seen by him as he says we are, then all our hardships would have their volume turned down. What sweet relief comes to us in all circumstances, facing anything, if we trust in God. No wonder the disciples cried out to Jesus, "Increase our faith!" (Luke 17:5).

Seeing the Wind

The house I grew up in was on a busy street in a busy neighborhood. We lived right next to a gas station and some fast-food restaurants. As a child, the voices and noises I would hear at night after I went to bed would plague my dreams. There was one particular night that I was absolutely positive I was hearing aliens right outside my window discussing my inevitable abduction. So I did what any self-respecting child would do in such a terrifying situation—I sprinted to get my mom. (It's common knowledge that aliens have no power over Earth's mothers.) She dismissed me the first few times, but eventually she

---

1   Douglas J. Moo, *Galatians* (Baker, 2013), on Gal. 5:22, Kindle.

came to my room to confront the nefarious off-worlders. Because my mom is courageous, she threw back my curtains and whipped open my window with no hesitation—she wasn't even armed. Suddenly the muffled conversation I'd been hearing became all too clear. I'm sure you'll all be relieved to know that the extraterrestrials turned out to be a drive-through employee across the street loudly discussing what a customer wanted on his sandwich.

When kids are afraid, they turn to their moms and dads. Children have faith in their parents. In other words, they rely on them. My kids look to me when they're scared. It's because they trust me. They trust me to tell them if there is a reason to be afraid. They trust me to protect them if there's danger. They trust me to know what to do. That is a kind of faith.

We see this same faith in the story of Jesus walking across the Sea of Galilee. When the disciples saw Jesus, they were scared. But Jesus reassured them and told them not to be afraid. So Peter said, "If it is you, command me to come to you on the water" (Matt. 14:28). Jesus replied, "Come" (14:29).

At this point, Peter got out of the boat and walked to Jesus on the water, but "when he saw the wind, he was afraid" (14:30). He began to sink and cried out to Jesus to save him. In that moment, Jesus "took hold of him" and said, "O you of little faith, why did you doubt?" (14:31).

Five times in Matthew, Jesus describes his disciples as people of "little faith" (6:30, 8:26, 14:31, 16:8, 17:20). There is no evidence of this term in any other ancient documents, so it seems that Jesus coined it himself. In Greek it is *oligopistos*, a combination of the word *oligos*, which means "few," "puny," or "brief," and the word we've been looking at, *pistis*, which means "faith." Jesus is making his own compound word or portmanteau, which blends two words to make a new one (like "brunch" or "hangry"). *Oligopistos* could mean "tiny trust," "no confidence," or even "brief belief." In other words, it could be describing an amount of trust (not much), a size of faith (puny), or a reliance on God for only short periods of time (brief). All these meanings were applicable to Peter in this circumstance.

The way Matthew describes Peter's fear is very interesting: he says that Peter was relying on Jesus until he "saw the wind." Peter was standing right in front of Jesus, experiencing a miracle, and yet he lost sight of Christ because he was looking at the wind, which scared him. Peter started on a faith journey toward Jesus, but he didn't make it far, and it didn't last long. He looked around him and began to fear that he was in danger. Peter was scared. This fear was understandable, but it was also needless. "O you of brief belief!"

In other words, Peter was looking at the wrong thing in the wrong way. He trusted Jesus, but his faith did not extend far enough to last through the storm. This is often what happens to us as parents. We have brief belief, little faith. I have seen many parents say they trust in God but have their faith shaken when things go awry. It's hard to remain steadfast when your surroundings are not firm.

Yet on the other hand, I have also seen parents endure the most tragic experience a family could imagine and still have an undaunted faith. Their confidence is resolute. That is the fruit of the Spirit. The fruit of the Spirit is not a tiny trust but a strengthening, growing, and long-term faith that is not easily shaken. Lord, grow it! Lord, multiply it! Lord, lengthen it! We cry out along with the disciples, "Increase our faith!" (Luke 17:5).

Faith means looking to Jesus when we are afraid and relying on Jesus when we are out of our depth. When we realize that we are afraid, when we become aware that we are operating out of fear, we can be sure that we are not relying on God but looking at the wind instead. Faith is all about where you are looking for protection. We must ask for a strong and steadfast faith placed in God and nowhere else.

Like a scared child runs to a beloved parent, we are welcome to bring our fears to God, whom we know is never afraid. You will never see Jesus cower, tremble, or hide. You will also never hear Jesus struggle to trust the Father because the Father is trustworthy. When we rely on God, we are firmly anchored even in the middle of a storm.

I see something similar in my own family. My kids are confident about my care for them, and yet I know better. I can be easily overpowered. Our family's confidence would be much better placed in our God, who is all-powerful and all-knowing. When things fall apart, our confidence is anchored in God. We are "strong in the Lord and in the strength of his might" (Eph. 6:10).

There is no wind that is stronger than Jesus. Whatever form your opposition takes, Jesus will not be overpowered. Our souls are always secure with him. We can trust in Jesus always, in all ways.

That does not mean we will always be safe or that we will never suffer, but it does mean that we can rely on God even when we are in danger and even when we are suffering. James also reminds us that the trials we face that test us produce faith and other blessings for us too. Such trials are a means by which God increases, strengthens, and extends our faith. James says, "Count it all joy, my brothers, when you meet trials of various kinds, for you know that the testing of your faith produces steadfastness. And let steadfastness have its full effect, that you may be perfect and complete, lacking in nothing" (James 1:2–4). This is the hope of the parent who walks by the Spirit—that our confidence in God would not be brief belief. We would not have a fragile confidence that leaves room for shame, anxiety, or despair. Lord, help us be steadfast!

Seeing the Word

Before my kids knew how to swim, we took them to an indoor water park. One of my sons and I rode some tubes around a fast-moving lazy river. Somehow, when we came to the end of our loop, I was able to climb up the stairs with my tube to the exit, but he missed it. He and his tube kept whipping along, now without me by his side. There was no way for me to get to him. I had to wait for him to make the whole loop by himself before I could reach in for a rescue. Though he could not find me in the crowd, I could see him. I watched him the whole way. He was terrified. I wanted him to look at me. I wanted him to see me. I wanted to reassure him that he was not alone. That he was okay. That I was watching. That I would soon scoop him up and out of his predicament. When he finally saw me coming to get him, he was so relieved. He hugged me harder than ever when we reunited.

If we would only look for help from the Father, we would see that he has never lost us or forgotten us. If we would stop looking at the wind and look to Jesus, stop looking at the potential dangers and focus on our rescuer, we would see that we have nothing to fear. We are seen. We are loved. No one has wrested control of our life away from God.

It's when we lose sight of God that our doubts eat away at our courage and confidence and that our suffering seems meaningless. If we would keep our eyes on our heavenly Father instead of on the wind, our anxieties would melt away to peace. Despair would yield to joy. All our stress would be relieved by his love. We could endure anything.

In Psalm 121:1, the psalmist asks this question: "I lift up my eyes to the hills. From where does my help come?" The answer is "My help comes from the LORD, who made heaven and earth" (121:2). Is there anything in the world that is stronger than the one who made the world? No. This is why Christian parents put their faith in God and nowhere else—because he alone is mighty to save. As it says in Zephaniah 3:17,

> The LORD your God is in your midst,
>   a mighty one who will save;
> he will rejoice over you with gladness;
>   he will quiet you by his love;
> he will exult over you with loud singing.

God is with us. He is strong. He is glad and loving.

Of course, looking to Jesus instead of the wind sounds nice, but it might be hard to understand what that looks like in practical terms.

Paul can help us here. He tells us in Romans 10:17 that "faith comes from hearing, and hearing through the word of Christ." Instead of scrambling through this world wondering how we can protect ourselves, we must turn to God's word. We must read the Bible believing that God has something to say to us that we need to hear. We trust what he says is true. We turn to him in prayer, believing that he listens. We trust he hears us. We ask him to lead us and save us, believing that he doesn't just speak and hear but also cares and takes action. He is with us, and "if God is for us, who can be against us?" (Rom. 8:31). Why would God's people have anything to fear? Listen to God's reassurances to you, and tattoo them on the inside of your eyelids. He says in Isaiah 41:10,

> Fear not, for I am with you;
>> be not dismayed, for I am your God;
> I will strengthen you, I will help you,
>> I will uphold you with my righteous right hand.

In Deuteronomy 1:31, Moses reminds the people of God, "You have seen how the LORD your God carried you, as a man carries his son." That is the picture I want to have running through your mind when you are afraid. How does a father carry a son? When my sons were really little, I carried them in my arms, then on my shoulders, and as they got older, I carried them piggyback style. The Lord carries you like a father carries his son. Imagine that. God tells you to hop on his back because he's got you!

If God Could

One night when my sons were still very little, one of them asked during our nightly family discipleship time, "Why did God even make Satan? Seems like things would have been a lot better without him." It led to a great discussion, and I was really proud of his depth of thought.

I love that struggling with doubts and questions is welcome in Christianity. There's no fear that doubt will unravel your religion when you are sure your religion is true. When you believe that God's word is true, all questions are welcome. We can safely share our skepticism and wrestle with our misgivings.

Doubts can take many forms for Christians. We might struggle to accept theological tenets, have a hard time believing the miraculous events recorded in the Bible, or pray for healing only to feel as if we don't get an answer from God. An unanswered prayer or a cosmic injustice can test the strongest faith. A lot of the questions I hear boil down to some version of this: "If the world is broken and God is all-powerful, then why doesn't he fix what's broken?"

Oddly enough, sometimes I see doubt in my heart when God *answers* my prayers. I remember the surprise (and then guilt) I felt in my heart when I heard that one of my friends I had prayed for after he received a cancer diagnosis found out that the cancer had disappeared. This was exactly what I had asked God for, but a big part of me did not expect it. I was genuinely surprised. I prayed for God to do something specific and then assumed he would not. I thought I had placed my trust in God whether he cured my friend or not, but the skepticism in my heart revealed that I was not trusting God to do whatever he willed. Rather, I had already assumed he would not cure my friend. I prayed but had little faith.

I know I am not alone in this struggle for confidence in the God I say I trust. The Gospel of Mark tells us the story of a desperate father. He is heartbroken over his son's lifelong struggle with an evil spirit and how it has harmed him. All of us can relate to the feelings he must have navigated, that sense of desperation to see his son delivered. Maybe questions of why God would allow this or do this or ignore this were flitting around in his mind.

The father brings his son to the disciples for deliverance, and they cannot help him. It starts an argument that Jesus interrupts. The father says to Jesus, "If you can do anything, have compassion on us and help us" (Mark 9:22). Jesus replies, " 'If you can'! All things are possible for one who believes" (9:23). Then, "immediately the father of the child cried out and said, 'I believe; help my unbelief!' " (9:24).

Christians rely on God but not perfectly. We may believe that all things are possible, but we have trouble relying on God in all circumstances. We can all relate to this desperate father when he says, "I believe, but help me when I don't!" He doesn't just say, "Help my son," but, "Help my unbelief!" And we pray with him, "Where my faith is too small, help me. Where I struggle to endure, help me. Where I doubt, help me." We don't find more faith by turning inward. We find more faith by turning to God.

Also, notice what Jesus says to his disciples at the end of this story. They seemed to have lost confidence in what God might do through them, and they did not take the time to ask God for his help. After Jesus delivers the boy, the disciples ask Jesus why they did not have success in setting the boy free. Jesus says that nothing but prayer will work (9:29).

Here Jesus was not offering a secret strategy for this particular instance but making an important and broader point: He was inviting the disciples to see that prayer was their greatest strength, their sharpest tool, their unparalleled privilege—not a last resort. When you want to see God do something, ask him in faith.

Parents, we are home-free because we can pray. It's our first resort. Our best strategy. Prayer is our remedy. If we trust God, we pray to God for help. If we want more faith, we pray to God for more. We are free from fear because we have the attention of God. We pray and we trust his response.

Take a moment right now and think about what you want to say to God. While your hands and thoughts aren't busy, what comes to your mind? Imagine that your perfect heavenly Father is sitting across a table from you right now. His eyes are intensely focused on you. He is eager to hear what you have to say. What will you tell him? What will you ask him? What do you need from him? Spend some time talking to him.

A Prayer for Times of Fear

Heavenly Father, there are things in this world that frighten me. I treat the world you created as something you can't control. I lack trust in you, and I honestly forget that you care. My faith is so weak sometimes.

I believe you, Father, but help me in my unbelief. Where my faith has limits, push them. Where my trust is small, grow it. Where my belief is brief, extend it. I want to walk in courage and confidence with my eyes fixed on you. Help me focus on your word and ignore the winds of this world. Make me steadfast and fearless. Amen.

Reflection Questions

1. What fears do you have regarding your family?

2. How have you seen your family rely on you when they are scared?

3. How has facing fears helped you grow?

4. What part has doubt played in your faith journey?

5. If your child said to you, "I don't trust God to help us," how would you reply?

6. Read Isaiah 41:10: "Fear not, for I am with you; be not dismayed, for I am your God; I will strengthen you, I will help you, I will uphold you with my righteous right hand." If you did what God says in this verse and he did what he says he would, what would change in your heart and home?

The Lord will happiness divine
On contrite hearts bestow;
Then tell me, gracious God, is mine
A contrite heart or no?

I hear, but seem to hear in vain,
Insensible as steel;
If aught is felt, 'tis only pain
To find I cannot feel.

I sometimes think myself inclined
To love Thee, if I could;
But often feel another mind,
Averse to all that's good.

My best desires are faint and few,
I fain would strive for more!
But, when I cry, "My strength renew,"
Seem weaker than before.

Thy saints are comforted, I know,
And love Thy house of prayer!
I sometimes go where others go,
But find no comfort there.

Oh make this heart rejoice or ache!
Decide this doubt for me;
And, if it be not broken, break,
And heal it, if it be.

WILLIAM COWPER
"The Contrite Heart" (1779)

10

Gentleness

Relief from Conflict

WE ASSESS, AND WE TREAT. Every parent must triage sometimes. Kids in pain become our patients. Concerned, we ask, "Where does it hurt?" We lovingly implore, "Tell me what happened." We blow on an ouchie. We Band-Aid a scrape. We splint a broken limb. We ice a swelling ankle. We monitor a fever. We give medicine for sicknesses. We listen to hurt feelings. We hug them when they're lonely. We help them take deep breaths when they are upset.

Does a loving dad poke a bump on the head, press a splinter deeper, smack a broken bone, or take the bully's side? Does a gentle mom ridicule her child's hurt feelings or withdraw when her child feels alone? No. That is because loving someone makes us gentle with their pain. We comfort afflicted children. We treat what hurts with gentleness. We do all this because we want to solve problems and mend wounds.

Right now, where does your family hurt? Where is there tension? Who needs to reconcile? Division is not a fruit of the Spirit. The outworking of your faith is neither cruelty nor vengeance. Every family experiences conflict, so every family needs to practice reconciliation. And the pain of conflict is relieved through gentleness.

How would you respond if Jesus asked you, "Where does it hurt?" or if your heavenly Father lovingly whispered, "Tell me what happened"? How does God handle your wounds? How do you think he addresses contentious families? God is gentle with our hurts. Walking with him will grow gentleness in us. A gentle touch leaves no scars. A gentle word leaves no wounds. A gentle look never rejects. A gentle look communicates concern. A gentle word mends what's damaged.

A gentle touch heals what hurts.

Not only is gentleness the best way to fix an already existing relational or emotional wound, but it is also the best way to prevent a new conflict. Gentleness is a remedy and a refuge—curative and preventive. It restores health, and it helps maintain health.

We all have scars from past wounds. I've been yelled at when a gentle answer would have turned away my wrath, and I have yelled in return. I've been mocked for defending myself and been told to toughen up when I'm hurting, but a little nurture would have restored me more quickly. I've been left out when friends are grouping up, and I know a gentle acknowledgment would have reassured me. In a thousand ways about a thousand things, I've been told not to feel the way I feel when a moment of gentle empathy would have done a lot more to serve me. In a thousand ways about a thousand things, I've told my own kids not to feel the way they feel when a modicum of gentle empathy would have done a lot more to serve them.

What if when we were most tempted to be vicious, we were gentle instead? What if when we felt most justified to criticize, we gently corrected? What if when we felt excused to lash out, enact vengeance, antagonize, cause pain, or provoke our children, we tempered the strength of our response or approach? Gentleness ends conflicts by mending family tensions, and it prevents conflicts by refusing to launch attacks.

Meekness, Not Weakness

The first time one of my sons tried to crack an egg, it didn't go very well. Or it went too well, depending on how you look at it. The egg definitely cracked, but not knowing how much strength to apply led to more of an explosion than a controlled yolk extraction. Egg innards went everywhere, and shell shrapnel spread far and wide.

Anyone can crack an egg. Dropping it from even a small height will smash it. But to crack an egg properly, to get the egg out of its shell without a mess, requires a wise application of strength, a practiced touch. That's gentleness. It's not feebleness or powerlessness or inaction but applying the right amount of force. It's having a delicate touch with fragile situations or people.

Many think of gentleness as weakness, but gentleness is a wise application of strength, not a lack of strength. Jesus is meek, but he is never weak. He uses his power in a controlled way, and we must learn from his example. People, especially children, are often more fragile than we think. How do you handle something that is precious and brittle? Gently.

Anyone can hurt feelings. You don't have to be powerful to hurt. Anyone can cause conflict in a relationship. It doesn't take a lot of talent to cause strife. But the ability to address hard things and not smash a relationship requires one to skillfully use one's power.

Sometimes we do need to say hard things. We need to address behavior that requires correction, or we need to communicate how we've been hurt. But we can do this either by attacking others and thus driving us even further from our goal of restoration or by offering a gentle word and thus sharing what needs to be said without creating collateral damage.

Our homes are perfect examples of these situations. As parents, we often need to respond to someone who is in an elevated emotional state. And matching or even exceeding such negative emotions rarely defuses a conflict. God says that "a soft answer turns away wrath" (Prov. 15:1). A gentle answer is a governed response that lovingly considers how our words and sentiments can mend what is broken and not cause more harm.

If you are married and you have to say something tough to your spouse, what is your go-to method? Is it screaming? Name-calling? Nagging? Undermining? Disrespecting? Being condescending?

If your children hurt your feelings, how do you speak to them about it? By humiliating them? Guilt-tripping? Berating?

You can't fix a broken heart with a toothbrush. It's nonsensical. It's the wrong tool. You can't dress a wound with a sledgehammer. You can't stitch a cut with a wrench. Likewise, you can't restore a broken relationship by pretending everything is okay or by throwing around insults. Really listen to what I'm saying here. You cannot truly apologize with an excuse. You can't make amends through a vengeful spirit. You can't take responsibility by shifting blame.

So what *is* the right tool for addressing conflict? It's gentleness. A loving, delicate consideration of others. Words that soothe instead of inflame. Tones that calm and respect and consider instead of contradicting or trying to conquer. Yet responding this way in times of conflict will take a degree of mental strength and emotional regulation you feel you aren't capable of in the moment. That is why you need to walk with the Spirit. Doing this will grow you into a person with governed power. It will make you a reconciler, a peacemaker.

Christ's Cooking and Cleaning

God's gentleness is often displayed through condescension. To condescend is to lower yourself in a humble manner in order to be considerate and accommodating. It's humble. In contrast, for a human to be condescending is to make others feel low by arrogantly patronizing them. It's prideful.

There is a condescending tone I use with my kids sometimes, in my worst moments, that if I used it with anyone else on planet Earth would be appalling. It's a rude "That was dumb, and I know better" tone that is all too common for me. If I saw a stranger spill his coffee and I blurted out, "What were you thinking? Put a lid on it!" it would startle onlookers. Or if I saw someone not finish her meal at a restaurant and I shared a quick "What a waste! Look how I clean my plate," I wouldn't win any friends.

Our culture accepts such levels of patronizing from moms and dads, but Christian parents are called to a higher standard. If we speak to our children in condescending ways, it reveals that we have a worldly idea of leadership: "I'm in charge. I'm up here. You're down there."

There is a better way than following the world's standard—the way we see in Jesus. Humble gentleness is something that we take for granted in Jesus. Though Jesus is perfect and all authority on heaven and earth has been given to him, during his earthly ministry he never acted condescendingly, and he was more than willing to demonstrate how kingdom leaders should be quick to condescend. He is never sinfully prideful, and he is always lowly and meek.

Of all the words that Jesus could use to describe himself, he chose "gentle and lowly" (Matt. 11:29). This means that he uses his strength carefully and that he is willing to make himself low for the sake of others. The ultimate leader, who has all authority, demonstrated gentleness and humility.

From Jesus's example we see clearly that leadership in the kingdom of God is different from leadership in the world. In Luke 22:25, Jesus says that worldly leaders will use their positions of authority to "exercise lordship over" their inferiors. Worldly leaders use a position of authority to get what they want or make others feel low. Parents are some of the worst offenders in this. But Jesus says, "It shall not be so among you" (Matt. 20:26)! If you want to be great in the kingdom of God, if you want to be a great leader, if you want to use your position of authority (such as mom or dad) in a kingdom manner, you must use your position to serve others.

Consider how this principle was displayed at the Last Supper, where a conflict was brewing between Jesus and Peter. Jesus tells Peter that he has been praying for Peter to have a faith that won't fail because Satan "demanded" to have him (Luke 22:31), but Peter swears he will never abandon Jesus, even if everyone else does. Then Jesus not only denies the truth of Peter's statement but also says that before the next morning, Peter will swear three times that he doesn't even know Jesus. Between two regular people, this might have led to a big "How dare you?" blowup.

But that is not the relationship Jesus and Peter had. Just before their conversation, Jesus demonstrates to Peter what it truly means to serve in order to be great by being willing to condescend. Knowing Peter will publicly deny Jesus multiple times, Jesus still washes Peter's feet. Imagine that you know that your child is about to disobey you, betray you, and disown you in the worst way, and then you still get down on your hands and knees to wash his feet. That's governed power. That is a gentle approach to conflict. Jesus is right, of course, about the mistakes Peter will make, but he is willing to do what it takes to cleanse and serve Peter even when Peter doesn't deserve it.

Then, after the resurrection, Jesus restores his relationship with Peter in a very unexpected way. He navigates their conflict with delicate love. Though Peter still experiences emotional pain and grief, the tact Jesus uses in this situation is amazing.

Does he give Peter a cold shoulder? Does he withdraw and pout? Does he make passive-aggressive comments? Does he lord it over him with an "I told you so"? Does he yell at him? Does he berate, humiliate, or reject him? No. Unlike us in many circumstances, he doesn't do any of those things.

Instead, Jesus cooks Peter breakfast and takes him on a walk. Jesus wants to talk through it. Jesus wants to restore what has been broken. He doesn't promise that everything is going to be okay or excuse Peter's behavior. If anything, he promises that Peter will suffer for following him. Peter will end up going "where [he does] not want to go" (John 21:18). But in gentleness and love, Jesus invites Peter into a reconciled relationship.

Imagine if we followed Jesus's example. What if when your child or your spouse wronged you, you responded by serving him or her, not passive-aggressively but out of sincere love? What if when your children disobeyed, you didn't berate them but blessed them, not canceling all consequences but eliminating escalating hostility? What if you addressed every conflict with a gentle tone and a heart to serve, cooking and cleaning for the one who broke your trust?

What if when people in your family hurt you, you didn't ask yourself, "How can I avoid them?" or "How can I get back at them?" but rather "How can I serve them?" Or even "I wonder what they want for breakfast?" Jesus made a grilled fish breakfast for Peter. One of my favorite things nineteenth-century pastor Charles Spurgeon ever said was "There is hardship in everything except eating pancakes."[1] A few pancakes prepared with a servant's heart can do more to ease family tension than a short stack of defensive arguments doled out by a selfish heart. Jesus starts addressing Peter's betrayal of him by choosing to condescend. He finds a way to serve. In this case, he makes breakfast for a man who has worked all night.

What if, like Jesus, you invited the one who hurt you to go on a walk and talk it out? Where could you go that would give you a chance to have a calm, reconciling conversation? This is the fruit of walking by the Spirit. You respond to conflict with gentleness that will bring reconciliation. Restored relationships rarely result from winning arguments. Restoration is accomplished through sincere love and service, compassion for the humanity in the other person, humbly owning our own contribution to any conflict, forgiving, refusing to hold others' contribution against them, and committing to do better together. The tension in your home is relieved through humility and gentleness.

Gentleness and Rock-Solid Boundaries

I have helped a lot of people consider setting up appropriate boundaries in their life, often with extended family members. When emotional

---

1   C. H. Spurgeon, *John Ploughman's Pictures* (Philadelphia, 1896), 193.

wounds are still open and there is a lot of anger, resentment, or lack of safety, boundaries are critical.

For those who have suffered under abuse or manipulation, there is a fear that being gentle will allow someone to take advantage of them. But being gentle does not mean granting others permission to extort or exploit you. Being gentle does not mean becoming a doormat. If someone attempts to take advantage of your calm and gentle approach to conflict, it does not mean that you need to stoop to that person's level but indicates that it's time to set up some rock-solid boundaries.

When I first started dating my wife, we set up some firm relational boundaries. Yelling, name-calling, and gossiping about one another were all off-limits. Boundaries can be as simple as those, with spouses establishing preferences on how they'll handle conflict. Of course, some boundaries are much more serious and weighty. Boundaries can be as significant as not talking about a certain topic until one of the parties gets help with a particular issue, not spending time together until one party commits to getting help, or having no contact at all except through a mediator.

Consider what Paul says to his protégé Timothy:

> There will come times of difficulty. For people will be lovers of self, lovers of money, proud, arrogant, abusive, disobedient to their parents, ungrateful, unholy, heartless, unappeasable, slanderous, without self-control, brutal, not loving good, treacherous, reckless, swollen with conceit, lovers of pleasure rather than lovers of God, having the appearance of godliness, but denying its power. Avoid such people. (2 Tim. 3:1–5)

We are called to love everyone, but the Bible also warns us that some people, in some circumstances, should be avoided. That is a biblical boundary. You can keep loving them, forgive them, hope for their sanctification, and even navigate conflict with them, but it does not mean that you owe someone who is abusive, heartless, brutal, or treacherous access to you. Gentleness and boundaries are not mutually exclusive. You can be lowly, meek, humble, and forgiving and still protect yourself at the same time. Even if someone who hurts you repents and you forgive him, you do not owe him an opportunity to hurt you again. Sincere repentance and genuine forgiveness do not create debt. If you are facing any of these situations, please ask a person you trust to help you establish some firm boundaries.

Gentleness and Discipline

There are a lot of bad behaviors that bother me, but nothing gets under my skin more than being lied to. When my kids do something I find to be particularly appalling, like being deceptive, I instinctively pump up my sternness and harshness. It's almost as if I believe that gentle words could not possibly communicate the severity of the situation, that tyranny is the highest and most effective way to wield power. I try to be scarier to get my point across. When I want desperately to be obeyed or respected, I parent like a bully.

A gentle parent, however, is not an impotent parent. Gentleness does not lead to surrendering in every conflict. We don't have to wave the white flag in every disagreement to be lowly. Gentle parents still enact discipline and still offer firm correction, but they shape their child with fine-grit sandpaper rather than a hammer. Gentle parents still expect to be honored and respected, but they don't rule with an iron fist or maintain order through threats.

Gentle correction is never done out of anger. Gentle discipline is never vulgar or severe. Gentle training is always done with the best interests of the child in mind. It comes from a loving heart and a self-controlled parental response to misbehavior. This fruit of the Spirit is our greatest tool in calling our child to something better.

My children and I can both tell the difference between me disciplining them humbly and gently and correcting them pridefully and harshly. On the one hand, pride demands obedience, but it comes at the cost of a relationship. It establishes me and my kids as opposing forces and attempts to bend their wills to mine. On the other hand, humility corrects while building mutual trust, putting us both on the same side. Being on the same side as your child is a way to serve them, and gentle discipline is done out of a heart to serve.

Unlike a gentle approach, a harsh rebuke leads to feelings of rejection. A gentle rebuke is done in the hope of restoration. Paul calls Timothy to correct people gently when he writes,

> The Lord's servant must not be quarrelsome but kind to everyone, able to teach, patiently enduring evil, correcting his opponents with gentleness. God may perhaps grant them repentance leading to a knowledge of the truth, and they may come to their senses and escape from the snare of the devil, after being captured by him to do his will. (2 Tim. 2:24–26)

Similarly, in his letter to the Galatians, Paul reminds us both how to approach the sin of others with gentleness and how to be cautious about our own sin. He writes, "Brothers, if anyone is caught in any transgression, you who are spiritual should restore him in a spirit of gentleness. Keep watch on yourself, lest you too be tempted" (Gal. 6:1). Moms and dads are not only in positions of authority but are also under authority—the authority of God and the church. We need gentle correction regarding how we lead our families and follow our God.

When we don't know quite how to feel about how we are doing, we become insecure. Insecurity can make any critique feel like an attack. But the truth is that not all feedback is an accusation. We must be able to hear and call for change without giving or taking offense.

Everyone needs to be sanctified, to become more and more like Jesus. For our children, setting them on "the way [they] should go" (Prov.

22:6) involves stopping them from going in the way they shouldn't or helping them get off that road if they've already started on it. When Jesus witnesses a woman who has been caught in adultery, he does not stoop down to pick up a rock and throw the first stone at her. Rather, he disperses her accusers and says, "Neither do I condemn you; go, and from now on sin no more" (John 8:11). Notice that he does not condemn her but also does not leave her in her sin. What a gentle blessing to hear and receive, what a gentle gift to say and to offer the words "I do not condemn you; I forgive you. Now go, and don't do it again"!

God is gentle, but he does not coddle. God disciplines those he loves, and he tells us that discipline will not be fun (Heb. 12:6, 11). We can correct gently, but that does not mean that our kids will delight in our discipline. We want righteousness in, from, and for our family, and that means we will have difficult conversations even though we are still leading with gentleness.

Turning the Heart

At the very, very end of the Old Testament, the prophet Malachi says that at the coming of Elijah (fulfilled in John the Baptist) and the arrival of the "day of the LORD," God "will turn the hearts of fathers to their children and the hearts of children to their fathers" (Mal. 4:5–6). This is a sign that the power of the Messiah will restore and reconcile families. The broken family that's mended is a work of God.

Many children, sometimes repeatedly, will turn their hearts away from their parents. There will also be times when it feels as if the hearts of husbands and wives turn away from each other. And this pulling in opposite directions creates tension. To relieve such tension, these hearts must be turned back toward each other. Imagine a tug-of-war with your child on one side and you on the other. As long as you keep pulling in opposite directions, the tension will not be relieved. One of you may win by being stronger than the other, but the only way to relieve the tension is to go toward each other instead of away.

Ending conflicts in a gentle way will start with some very important commitments. The first step toward each other comes from taking responsibility for all your own sins. You own 100 percent of your portion of the conflict without excuse, without defensiveness, and without minimizing. Ask them what hurts, listen well, and own every ounce of what's true. The second step is to hold nothing against the other person. Forgive without bitterness, resentment, or entitlement. Give the benefit of the doubt, assuming the best. Let go of any sin against you that is sincerely confessed.

Take some steps to do all this right now. Who do you currently have conflict with? Your parents? Your kids? Your spouse? Start the reconciliation process by owning all you can and holding nothing against the other person. Do this genuinely and gently, and you'll find that your hearts will start to turn toward one another. You'll be able to calmly address wounds, establish appropriate boundaries, and reconcile. The tension in your family will be relieved when you come gently toward one another.

A Prayer for Times of Conflict

Heavenly Father, there is division in my home right now. Protect me from being the one that drives us further apart. Teach me how to address hurt. When I am hurt, help me heal. When I hurt others, help me reconcile with them and mend what I've broken.

Train me to own my mistakes. Give me grace in my heart for those who have wronged me. Give me the strength to create and maintain the right boundaries in my life. Please be gentle with me as you correct me and cultivate that gentleness in me so that I can be like you. Amen.

Reflection Questions

1. When have you been less than gentle lately?

2. Where do you see conflict in your family?

3. Do you need to establish better boundaries?

4. How can you serve someone you are in conflict with?

5. The next time your child does something you don't like, what could you say that would be firm but gentle?

6. What sin do you need to own up to, and what sin are you holding against someone else that you can let go of?

Oh for a faith that will not shrink,
Though pressed by every foe;
That will not tremble on the brink
Of any earthly woe;

A faith that shines more bright and clear
When tempests rage without;
That when in danger knows no fear,
In darkness feels no doubt;

That bears, unmoved, the world's dread frown,
Nor heeds its scornful smile;
That seas of trouble cannot drown,
Nor Satan's arts beguile;

A faith that keeps the narrow way
Till life's last hour is fled,
And with a pure and heavenly ray
Lights up a dying-bed!

WILLIAM HILEY BATHURST
"For Victorious Faith" (1831)

11

Self-Control

Relief from People Pleasing

IF MY KIDS WERE IN CHARGE of our family right now, we'd have ice cream or cookies at every meal. Actually, we'd have ice cream *and* cookies for every meal. We would eat a lot more pizza, and our vegetable intake would plummet. We'd see their friends all the time, but we would never do homework. Our video game and movie budget would skyrocket. There would be no more bedtime and no more alarm clocks. Chores would be a thing of the past. (Except for me. I'd still have dishes and laundry and other things to clean as they saw fit.) If my kids were in charge, there wouldn't be any more rules about screens, devices, or phones. I'd spend our retirement savings and even go into debt so we could have a trampoline and a pool and more pets and a multitude of huge, elaborate, lavish Lego sets.

What would your home life be like if your children were completely in charge? What would you have for dinner? How would your kids want to spend your money? What would they want to do every day?

If your kids oversaw whether you read the Bible together as a family, would it ever happen? If your kids decided where you went to church, would good doctrine be on their list of nonnegotiables? If your kids decided *if* you went to church, would you ever go? If your children set the ground rules for behavior, apologies, and reconciliation, how would etiquette shift in your home?

If your kids were in charge, how would they treat you differently? Would they honor you with their decisions, or would they find more ways for you to degrade yourself to honor them? If your children ruled your life, would they serve you or just expect to be served?

Kids for Kings

Children are wonderful. I love kids. But they make terrible masters. When children are in charge, they make childish decisions. If they had unlimited authority, most kids would become tyrants. Even the sweetest kids can become bullies if they're given enough power. It's rare to find a child who is adept at self-denial and selflessness. Thus, being "childish" is usually associated with the opposite—indulgence and selfishness.

I've seen families operate as if the wishes of the child are the most important consideration for a parent. But that is not a great way to develop resilience, maturity, and godliness in the next generation. If kids only do what they want to do and get whatever they want to get, what will form in them is not godliness but entitlement. If we conform to the wishes of our children, if we surrender our wisdom for the sake of a child's opinion, we might delight them and even make our own lives temporarily easier, but we are not serving or discipling them well.

Praise God that kids are not our masters! In Christ, our families have self-control, not kid control.

The word "self-control" makes it sound as if God might be saying, "We are our own masters!" That is not, however, what the Spirit cultivates in us. It's way better than that. Truly. If we ourselves became the master, it would be no better than kids being in charge. And what kind of freedom would it be if we were freed from one tyrant only to replace him with another? No, we are not our own masters either. Rather, God is our Master, and the Spirit helps us obey him, which leads to the flourishing of all life around us.

As your Master, God gives you strength to face temptations and leads you to choose what is good, even if it leads to a harder life. The gift of self-control is given to bless you. You don't have to do the sinful things that seem right to you. In Christ, we can throw off that sin that so easily entangles and pursue a better way to live—God's way.

The preoccupation with mastery goes back to the lie that Eve believed in the garden of Eden. Eve thought that being like God, replacing God, would be better for her. She indulged her sinful desires and rejected God's authority in her life. But that did not emancipate her—it enslaved her to sin as her master.

Self-control is the emancipating power of the Spirit that sets us free not to master ourselves but to be able to say that we submit to the best Master, Christ. Self-control brings relief from being under the rule of anyone but King Jesus. God's Spirit strengthens our willpower to refuse to obey anyone else but God. In Christ, sin and our selfish desires are no longer our masters. Jesus alone is our King. What a sweet relief. If our heart desires sin, we don't have to follow it because the Spirit gives us self-control. If the world pressures us to wander from Christ, we don't have to listen because the Spirit gives us self-control. The fruit of the Spirit is freedom from oppressive masters who tempt us to sin.

Overall, self-control comes from a God-given desire to do what God desires and a God-given strength to honor God in what we do. It frees us from a desire to disobey God and the detriment that comes from dishonoring God with our lives. You have one Master, and he is the best.

Holy Stubbornness

I've always thought that hot dogs are delicious, but when I was a kid, I hated eating the ends. They looked like belly buttons to me, and I thought they were disgusting. I would eat the whole thing except the last little stub, which I would leave on my plate. One day, this led to a big battle between me and my parents. They told me I could not eat another morsel of any other food until I finished off the hot dog. They were serious. But I was too. I dug in my heels and went on a hunger strike. Meanwhile, they made me carry the hot dog end around in a ziplock bag everywhere we went until I surrendered to eating it. While we were driving somewhere as a family, my older brother got so sick of the power struggle that when my parents weren't looking, he grabbed the bag out of my hands, threw it out of the van window, and declared, "Adam ate the rest of the hotdog!" It was a lie, but we all got what we wanted. I don't remember how long I had carried it around, but I do know that if it weren't for my brother, I might still have that gross frankfurter navel in my pocket today. *Never surrender!*

I've listened to many parents share their struggles with strong-willed children. It's a very real predicament. When a child is stubborn and defiant, parents can feel helpless and frustrated. No one wants a foolishly belligerent child. You can give your kid some broccoli, but you can't make him eat it. You can set up a playdate with friends, but you can't force your child to share her toys. You can tell your teens what's good for them, but you can't force them to believe you.

Yet as much as many forms of obstinance are totally undesirable in a child, if we are raising kids the way God called us to, we actually want to foster and cultivate a resolute, holy stubbornness. We want to raise our kids to be defiant. Yes, we want rebellious children. We are trying our best to form strong-willed children. Stick with me.

As parents who follow Jesus, we are trying to develop a stubbornness in our kids when it comes to overcoming sin. In whatever ways that the world is opposed to the things of God, we want our kids to choose God instead of the world. We want to raise children who are "blameless and innocent, children of God without blemish in the midst of a crooked and twisted generation, among whom you shine as lights in the world" (Phil. 2:15). Godly kids will stand out. They will stand rooted and firm even against the torrent of a world headed in the wrong direction. They will have to be headstrong and thick-skinned to follow Christ in a generation that does not love God. When the cultural current is strong, we want our children to be anchored to God's word. We want our families to be daring and bold because our way of life is far from fashionable.

Admittedly, this is not a super popular way to parent. As a parent, then, if we want to lead our families in a godly way while living in a godless culture, we will have to be just as stubborn and unwavering as a strong-willed child. That is not easy for us. But God empowers us to swim upstream. We don't have to let our kids date the way the world dates, use technology the way the world uses technology, or turn a blind eye to sin the way the world does.

Sometimes I hate sticking out. Worse than that, I hate being left out. But as much as I hate being humiliated or snubbed, I like those feelings for my kids even less. There have been times when making a different decision from other parents has been costly for my children. My kids have missed some social gatherings. They've missed some peer-to-peer communications. They've missed some inside jokes with their classmates. They have missed a lot, honestly. But I believe that because of those decisions we made as a family, they have gained much more than they missed.

We are not only protecting them but also fostering a readiness to feel different and strange in a world that is not our home. Here the Griffins "have no lasting city, but we seek the city that is to come" (Heb. 13:14). There is a pattern and a purpose that this world has to offer, and it is not what I want for my family. In this world, we will face many obvious and subtle enemies of the cross. Paul says that "their end is destruction, their god is their belly, and they glory in their shame, with minds set on earthly things. But our citizenship is in heaven, and from it we await a Savior, the Lord Jesus Christ" (Phil. 3:19–20). In many ways, if my family follows Jesus, we will feel like foreigners in our own neighborhood. Our family walks a narrower way.

The pressure to conform as a parent can be overwhelming. What has become "normal" to do or to believe is not always godly. It takes a lot of self-control and discipline to continue to battle the accommodations that the culture demands and expects.

I don't always like the feeling of being weird, but for the sake of Christ, I know that my family has been set apart from the world, and I wouldn't have it any other way. I have grown to embrace it. My family is strange to some people. I am an unusual dad trying to raise uncommon kids. My family makes what others think are weird decisions to honor God with our choices and actions. For that, I will never be embarrassed or sorry.

I want to raise kids who are dogmatic and say that they are not of the world just as Jesus is not of the world (John 17:16) and that they are "not ashamed of the gospel" (Rom. 1:16). Jesus says that we cannot have more than one master (Matt. 6:24). We don't have to do what the world wants. My God grows in us the discipline of self-control and frees us from the people-pleasing pressure to meet the expectations of someone who is not our master.

If we walk in step with the Spirit, he will lead us in being strong-willed children of God. We will not obey the desires of the flesh. Why would we return to that yoke of slavery?

The Weak-Willed Parent

In my student ministry days, I used to take high school students camping. One year I took two of the teenagers I was discipling on a canoe. At a split in the river, we made a wrong turn upstream. Don't ask me how. The first clue should have been how much harder it became to make progress. You'd think the difficulty of rowing against the current would have been enough to wake me to my mistake, but I have an astounding ability to make wrong turns in life without noticing. My absentmindedness is pretty impressive compared to most people. The second clue should have been how many canoes we passed going the other way. It literally took a stranger asking me why we were headed upstream before I realized we might not be headed in the right direction. Turning the canoe around and going with the flow was a totally different experience. We felt as if we were flying! It takes a lot more effort, determination, and strength to go against the current than with it.

As common as it is to talk about the difficulty of dealing with a headstrong child, I hear parents discuss far less often how easy it is to be a weak-willed parent. I see it, though. I see it. All the time.

I see Christian parents making decisions about what their family owns, how their family speaks, and what their family does or does not do that are no different from the godless culture around them. It is so easy to conform to the cultural current of the world or to give in to the selfish whims of a child.

Of all the struggles we talk about in this book, this is the most insidious and invisible challenge. Its stealth is what makes it especially dangerous. We know when we are anxious or ashamed. We have a sense of when we are growing in bitterness or entering conflict. It's harder to sense when we are struggling with being weak-willed, giving in to pressure from peers, or making choices to please people instead of God. It can be very difficult for us to notice when we have slipped into following other masters. That's why God describes it as a trap. He says that the "fear of man lays a snare" (Prov. 29:25). A snare is a trap that is hidden. You fall into it unexpectedly. When we live our lives making decisions based on what we think will please the people around us, as if they were our masters, we step into danger.

Often, parenting in the most popular or culturally acceptable way feels okay because it's easy to find validation in making the same decisions the families around us are making. Going with the flow of the families around us seems right. Doing what our community, kids, or our own heart wants feels great. Therein lies the trap. It's just easier. But it's easier and dangerous. We need relief from what's easy and even what's preferable to our worldly passions.

Jesus says that "the gate is wide and the way is easy that leads to destruction, and those who enter by it are many" (Matt. 7:13). And Proverbs reminds us that "there is a way that seems right to a man, but its end is the way to death" (Prov. 14:12). When we conform to the godless world around us, we will operate in a way that seems right, that is "normal" and common, but it will not lead to righteousness and holiness for our family.

But here is the good news. You do not have to surrender to the whims of any earthly master. Paul appeals to, literally pleads with, Christians to "not be conformed to this world, but be transformed by the renewal of your mind, that by testing you may discern what is the will of God, what is good and acceptable and perfect" (Rom. 12:2). The fruit of the Spirit is self-control. Being led by the Spirit fosters incredible strength in you. You can row upstream. You can run uphill. You can parent differently, set free from the oppression of unholy masters and the desire to fit in and gain approval. When you want to just float along with however the culture is going, you can resist that urge. You are relieved from the cultural pressure to parent in a way that compromises what you are called to in Christ.

We have an appetite for sin, but sin is not our master. We face a culture that does not point us to Christ, but our culture is not our master. We have a heart that is hostile toward the ways of God, but we are not our own master. Our Master is God, and he gives us the strength to follow him.

The Freedom of Protection

When I was a kid, nothing scared me like sharks. After I saw a movie scene in which sharks were released into a swimming pool to attack the main character, it haunted me every time I tried to swim. I was always on high alert, even in an indoor pool. My swim instructors always wondered why I seemed to be sprinting every lap. Better safe than sorry, I thought.

Even as an adult, I have no desire to be one of those people who get into the ocean to see sharks. I find no pleasure in masochistic tourism. There's a certain thrill-seeking crowd who churns the water with fish guts and then lowers themselves into a "shark cage" so that they can get close to these sharp-toothed, dead-eyed underwater monsters. No thank you.

If you saw a shark cage out of the water, you would think it might be a portable prison. All its walls are made of metal bars. It's designed almost exactly like a jail cell. The difference is that it is made to keep something dangerous out, not to keep someone dangerous trapped inside.

Proverbs tells us that "a man without self-control is like a city broken into and left without walls" (Prov. 25:28). A city without walls is vulnerable. It would be a dangerous place to be. It's a place without any protections.

When my family rides in our car, we buckle up our seat belts. When my kids were really small, we buckled our babies into infant car seats, strapped in like we were about to launch into space, and laid them down to sleep in a little baby prison we called a crib. When my kids ride bikes today, they wear helmets. When we ride roller coasters, we lower the lap bar. When we've done high-rope zip lines, we've worn harnesses. All these restrictions are put in place to protect us. They exist to support our freedom and allow for fun, not to take it away. They are limits that liberate.

Sometimes we confuse the purpose of laws and limits. When someone creates restrictions for us, we may feel as though we are being robbed of our freedoms, as though we've been put in a jail cell. But God says true freedom comes from living within good limits. James literally calls God's law the "law of liberty," the restrictions that set you free (James 1:25). Like a shark cage, God gives us limits to protect us from something dangerous outside. He is not robbing us of our freedoms and saying, "You can't just do whatever you want." He is providing loving limits that create freedom for us. He gives us a better Master, himself, not to take away our basic rights but to liberate us from the harm that comes from following a sinful leader, whether that be ourselves or someone else. Christ has set us free not just by breaking the bars of our jail cells but by building a wall around us. There is no freedom found for us in walking through life unprotected. Our freedom is not walls knocked down but comfort inside the fortified city of God.

No one wants to be tied down, right? That's not freedom! Unless we are on a ship that's loose in a storm—then we want to be anchored. Beleaguered and endangered, we want to be stable. "Don't let us drift, Lord!"

No one wants to be "trapped" behind four walls and a locked door, right? That's not freedom. Unless there's a prowling lion outside seeking someone to devour. Then bar the door and shutter the windows.

There's a true freedom that is found only in dependence on God. When we do not rely on God, we are like an unanchored ship—our emotions, desires, and decisions being tossed here and there by the waves—and thus we become vulnerable, fickle, and unguarded.

In my home, I lock my doors at night. I don't do that to trap my family inside. I do that to keep out anyone who might want to do harm to my family or take something from us. I create physical limits to guard and protect. I have rules with my kids not to rob them of the joy they would otherwise experience but to cultivate a godly environment for complete joy. Has this restriction robbed them of their liberty? No. Similarly, the fruit of self-control is how God fosters our freedom. He strengthens our restraint in order to free us from the powers and forces that seek to harm us or take from us. We trust our King, and we trust his laws.

The right posture before a king is to bow your head and lift your hands. This a position of submission. It implies that if the king wanted to take my life, then it is his. We lift our hands as if we are saying, "If you want to give me something, I'll take it. If I have something, it's at your service." Take a moment right now to bow your head and lift your hands. Sin is not your master. Your kids are not your kings. The world's morals are not your standard. Bow your head, lift your hands, and ask to be transformed by the renewing of your mind right this moment.

A Prayer for Relief from Worldly Pressure

Heavenly Father, my choices have been influenced by a world that does not love you. I have seen how my views and choices are being shaped by the pressures that come from people who are not following Jesus. Protect me from believing lies. Protect me from conforming to ungodly pressures.

Even if we are the only family that is still following you, help us stand strong. Help our family be strong-willed. Remind me that you are my only good and true Master. When my desires do not align with your will, guide them back to the narrow way you've called me to walk.

Give me limits that extend my freedom and my joy in obedience. Forgive me when I try to choose another master or ignore your restrictions. Teach me to delight in your ways. Amen.

Reflection Questions

1. If your kids were in charge of your family, how would it function?

2. What do you think God desires for your family?

3. What is a cultural trend in parenting that you know does not honor God?

4. Where do you feel as though you are tempted to conform to the world?

5. What families around you are also trying to raise their kids to follow Jesus? How can you do this together?

6. Galatians 1:10 says, "For am I now seeking the approval of man, or of God? Or am I trying to please man? If I were still trying to please man, I would not be a servant of Christ." If you applied this verse to your life right now, what would need to change?

Happy the home when God is there,
And love fills every breast;
Where one their wish, and one their prayer,
And one their heavenly rest.

Happy the home where Jesus' name
Is sweet to every ear;
Where children early lisp his fame,
And parents hold him dear.

Happy the home where prayer is heard,
And praise is wont to rise;
Where parents love the sacred Word,
And live but for the skies.

Lord, let us in our home agree
This blessed peace to gain:
Unite our hearts in love to thee,
And love to all will reign.

HENRY WARE
"Happy the Home When God Is There" (1846)

Conclusion

The Home-Free Home

I ONCE ASKED MY THREE SONS, "If you were a ghost and you could haunt any place that you like, what would you haunt?" One of my sons said, "Lambeau Field, so I could see the Packers play." The next son said, "McDonald's" (no explanation was offered). And my third son said, "I'd haunt my own house so I could stay with my family."

I want my home to be the greatest place on earth for my family. I hope we always want to be together. But whether my kids enjoy our home or not, I know that being part of a good, godly family comes from having a dad who walks by the Spirit. We want a home marked by the outcomes of our faith, the fruit of being with God, relieved from worldly burdens. That's my prayer for all of us who parent out of our union with Christ.

My friend Victor and I were talking about parenting from a place of Christian confidence and comfort, and he shared a C. S. Lewis quote with me from his science fiction novel *A Hideous Strength*, in which Lewis is describing his protagonist's difficulty with finding joy and peace. Lewis writes,

How did other people . . . find it so easy to saunter through the world with all their muscles relaxed and a careless eye roving the horizon, bubbling over with fancy and humour, sensitive to beauty, not continually on their guard and not needing to be? What was the secret of that fine, easy laughter which he could not by any efforts imitate? Everything about them was different. They could not even fling themselves into chairs without suggesting by the very posture of their limbs a certain lordliness, a leonine indolence. There was elbow-room in their lives, as there had never been in his.[1]

This sense of carefree confidence is what life with the Spirit cultivates. You can find this "easy laughter" through your walk with God. Rooted in the gospel, I want your parenting to be characterized by a holy "sauntering" and a godly "leonine indolence." Have you ever seen a lounging lion? He's at the top of the food chain. Unguarded. Unhurried. Unharried. Unworried. This is the image drawn by Lewis's brilliant turn of phrase "leonine indolence." It means to be at rest, relaxed, or calm like a lion. I want your parenting to have this kind of relaxed approach, rooted in your identity in Christ.

Made a mistake? You cast off what used to crush you. Someone's critiquing you? You receive what is helpful, are grateful for that, and let what's not fair or true roll right off your back. There's a lot to do? You consecrate your work as worship and don't feel overwhelmed because you love the people and the God you serve. Your world is crumbling? The gladness of your heart is not shaken since your hope is impervious. You realize that you can't control what is happening? You don't worry as you used to because you trust the one who is in charge. Your energy or enthusiasm is waning? You find renewed strength in the Almighty and in his word. No one's appreciating your hard work? You aren't bothered because that's not why you're doing it. You don't feel as though you are good enough? You know that God already knows all your failings and is pleased with you. Your fears are coming true? Your

---

1   C. S. Lewis, *That Hideous Strength* (Macmillan, 1946), 447.

faith outgrows your challenges. There's opposition coming from your kids? This is what you expected, so you're still strong and gentle. All the other parents are making different choices for their kids? You have no regrets for sticking with God over them.

You're walking by the Spirit, so you're always learning and growing in love, joy, peace, patience, kindness, goodness, faithfulness, gentleness, and self-control. Because you follow Jesus, there is something different about you. Your home is marked by a calming courage, a soothing freedom, and a welcome relief rooted in Christ. You've got room to grow, but even now you know that, no matter what, you're home-free.

God moves in a mysterious way
His wonders to perform;
He plants His footsteps in the sea
And rides upon the storm.

Deep in unfathomable mines
Of never-failing skill,
He treasures up His bright designs,
And works His sov'reign will.

Ye fearful saints, fresh courage take;
The clouds ye so much dread
Are big with mercy and shall break
In blessings on your head.

Judge not the Lord by feeble sense,
But trust Him for His grace;
Behind a frowning providence
He hides a smiling face.

His purposes will ripen fast,
Unfolding every hour;
The bud may have a bitter taste,
But sweet will be the flow'r.

Blind unbelief is sure to err,
And scan His work in vain;
God is His own interpreter,
And He will make it plain.

WILLIAM COWPER
"God Moves in a Mysterious Way" (1774)

General Index

Scripture Index

Also Available from Adam Griffin

Here is a book written for parents that focuses not on their inability, but on God's ability to help raise their children in the faith through a guided framework focusing on time, moments, and milestones.

For more information, visit **crossway.org**.